Audio Access Included

W9-BJA-908

BY TROY NELSON

Contents

To access audio visit:
www.halleonard.com/mylibrary
Enter Code
3066-8403-4314-7788

ISBN: 978-1-4234-1435-3

HAL•LEONARD®
CORPORATION

7777 W. BLUEMOUND RD. P.O. BOX 13819 MILWAUKEE, WI 53213

In Australia Contact:
Hal Leonard Australia Pty. Ltd.
4 Lentara Court
Cheltenham, Victoria, 3192 Australia
Email: ausadmin@halleonard.com.au

Copyright © 2007 by HAL LEONARD CORPORATION
International Copyright Secured   All Rights Reserved

No part of this publication may be reproduced in any form
or by any means without the prior written permission of the Publisher.

Visit Hal Leonard Online at
www.halleonard.com

AUDIO TRACKS
EXERCISES

All guitars by Doug Boduch

RHYTHM TRACKS

All drums by Scott Schroedl

INTRODUCTION

When my good friends at Hal Leonard first approached me about writing this book, they already had a title, *Guitar Aerobics*, and a topic, guitar technique, in mind. Other than those two details, however, they kindly gave me carte blanche to create the rest. One thing was certain: I did not want to introduce another run-of-the-mill technique book to the guitar-publications marketplace, one that was filled cover to cover with bland chromatic exercises that ran senselessly up and down the fretboard. Instead, I wanted to devise a guitar-technique book that at once helped the reader develop, improve, and maintain his/her guitar chops via musical examples that could be applied to real-world musical settings, from rock and blues to jazz and country. And most importantly, I wanted to create a book that was *fun*! Too often practice sessions become monotonous due to the lack of uninspired materials from which to learn. With *Guitar Aerobics*, that's no longer the case.

Guitar Aerobics is the ultimate workout program for guitarists, promoting guitar facility, increasing pick- and fret-hand speed and accuracy, and improving dexterity while at the same time increasing lick vocabulary. The 52-week program covers one indispensable guitar technique each day—*alternate picking* on Monday, *string skipping* on Tuesday, *string bending* on Wednesday, *arpeggios* on Thursday, *sweep picking* on Friday, *legato* on Saturday, and *rhythm* on Sunday—all of which are presented within the context of either an applicable guitar lick or an exercise that is considerably more musical than the chromatic exercises found in other technique books. Moreover, because each example fits into one of six musical styles—rock, blues, jazz, metal, country, or funk—once you've got the lick down cold, you can test drive it at your next jam session, whatever style of music you play.

Guitar Aerobics is systematically arranged so that each week the musical examples increase in difficulty. If you consider yourself a beginner, you can jump right into Week 1 and feel perfectly comfortable playing the material. Consequently, you'll have an entire calendar year of material—365 exercises—to practice! At approximately Week 18, the material is more appropriate for players of an intermediate level. And Week 36 marks the entry point for those players who possess considerable chops (i.e., advanced). If you fit in the last category, that's still 120 exercises to get through! *Guitar Aerobics* offers something for everyone.

Additionally, each exercise includes a brief description—origin, scale(s), rhythms, etc.—as well as a performance tip. And true to the book's "workout" theme, all of the exercises come with a practice routine that is divided into eight sets, each of which contains a specific tempo (e.g., 112 beats per minute) at which to play the exercise. Ten repetitions ("reps") are played per set, with the tempos increasing at various increments from one set to the next, depending on the exercise's musical style. For example, here's how to perform the Rock/Blues workout:

ROCK/BLUES WORKOUT

🔊 Rhythm Tracks 1–8

Set 1: 40 bpm x 10 reps   **Set 5:** 84 bpm x 10 reps
Set 2: 48 bpm x 10 reps   **Set 6:** 96 bpm x 10 reps
Set 3: 58 bpm x 10 reps   **Set 7:** 108 bpm x 10 reps
Set 4: 72 bpm x 10 reps   **Set 8:** 120 bpm x 10 reps

Each exercise is labeled with a genre and track listing, which together denote the workout you should follow.

Every musical example in *Guitar Aerobics* (365 in all) can be heard on accompanying audio online, with all of the 52 weeks separated onto individual tracks. Therefore, you can quickly cue up a specific lick to hear how it should sound. Tuning notes (low to high, E–A–D–G–B–E) are also included on the final audio track. The audio contains rhythm tracks (drums only) performed at a variety of tempos dictated by their respective genre, including straight rock/blues, blues shuffle, jazz swing, funk, country, and metal. So throw away your metronome—now you've got a real drummer to keep time!

If you devote just a few minutes of each day to practicing the examples in this book, I guarantee that you'll notice immediate improvements in your guitar technique. By the time 365 days have passed, your chops will be second to none. Personally, I noticed considerable improvement in my technique during the writing of this book—and I didn't follow the workout program! All that it takes is a little time, dedication, and determination. Good luck!

THE TECHNIQUES

As I mentioned previously, seven techniques—alternate picking, string skipping, string bending, arpeggios, sweep picking, legato, and rhythm—are covered in *Guitar Aerobics*, one technique for each day of the week. Although there are many guitar techniques that are *not* presented in this book, I believe these seven techniques are the most essential for guitarists. Mastering these techniques will reduce limitations and equip you with the tools necessary to achieve the goals you have set for yourself on the instrument.

Here, now, is a brief overview of the techniques presented in this book:

Alternate Picking: No technique is more prevalent—and of greater benefit—than alternate picking. A fundamental guitar technique, it can be applied to any musical context and is *the* technique that separates the men/women from the boys/girls. On these pages, the technique, a continuous alternation of downstrokes and upstrokes with your pick hand, is applied to everything from rock and blues to jazz and country.

String Skipping: Most commonly associated with rock and metal, string skipping is also quite useful when playing other forms of music. The predominant focus of the string-skipping examples in this book is that of single- and double-string skips within the context of blues, jazz, rock, and metal.

String Bending: These examples, which mostly consist of blues, country, and rock licks, feature quarter-step, half-step, and whole-step bends, as well as more sophisticated bends such as oblique, unison, compound, and pre-bends.

Arpeggios: Although an "arpeggio" in and of itself is not a technique, the coordination of right- and left-hand movements used to perform one certainly qualifies. The definition of an *arpeggio* is "a chord whose notes are played in rapid succession rather than simultaneously," and the examples herein illustrate that in practically every possible combination on the neck, from simple open position–chord combinations to advanced sweep-picking concepts. Which brings us to our next technique…

Sweep Picking: The polar opposite of alternate picking, sweep picking involves using one continuous down or upstroke to play two or more adjacent-string notes. Although most of the examples in *Guitar Aerobics* apply to rock and metal, you will find a few interesting examples of how to apply this technique to jazz and blues as well.

Legato: On the guitar, legato technique involves pull-offs, hammer-ons, slides, finger tapping, or any combination hereof. Basically, legato is any collection of two or more notes on the same string that isn't articulated with a succession of pick attacks. A wide variety of such licks is included on the following pages.

Rhythm: Much like an arpeggio, "rhythm" isn't a single technique, but rather a collection of techniques used to perform various functions as they relate to a specific rhythmic style. A few of the topics covered in *Guitar Aerobics* include basic strum patterns, open-chord arpeggios, boogie batterns, walking bass lines, and much more.

EXERCISE TRACK 1

MON

Exercise: #1   **Rhythm Tracks:** 9–16   **Technique:** Alternate Picking   **Genre:** Metal

Music Description: Performed exclusively in sixteenth notes on the first string, this lick makes its way up the neck by utilizing every note of the E harmonic minor scale (E–F♯–G–A–B–C–D♯).

Tip: Reverse your picking pattern after playing through the lick a few times, beginning with an upstroke.

0:00

TUE

Exercise: #2   **Rhythm Tracks:** 1–8   **Technique:** String Skipping   **Genre:** Rock/Blues

Music Description: This exercise is based in the root position of the A minor pentatonic scale (A–C–D–E–G) and skips a string between each note pair.

Tip: Throughout the figure, keep your index, middle, ring, and pinky fingers positioned at the fifth, sixth, seventh, and eight frets, respectively.

0:11

WED

Exercise: #3   **Rhythm Tracks:** 1–8   **Technique:** String Bending   **Genre:** Rock/Blues

Music Description: This descending lick is also based in A minor pentatonic and features whole-step bends on the second and third strings.

Tip: Reinforce each bend with fingers not directly performing the bend. For example, when executing the third-string bend in measure 1, reinforce your ring finger your middle and index fingers.

0:23

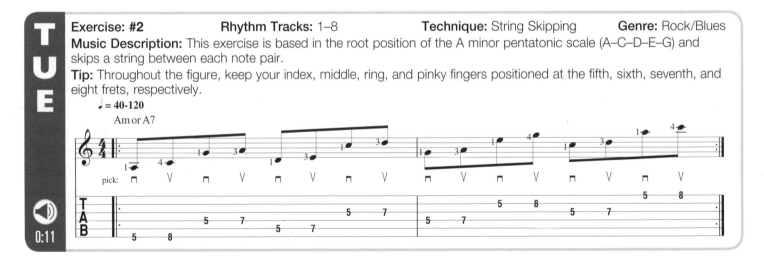

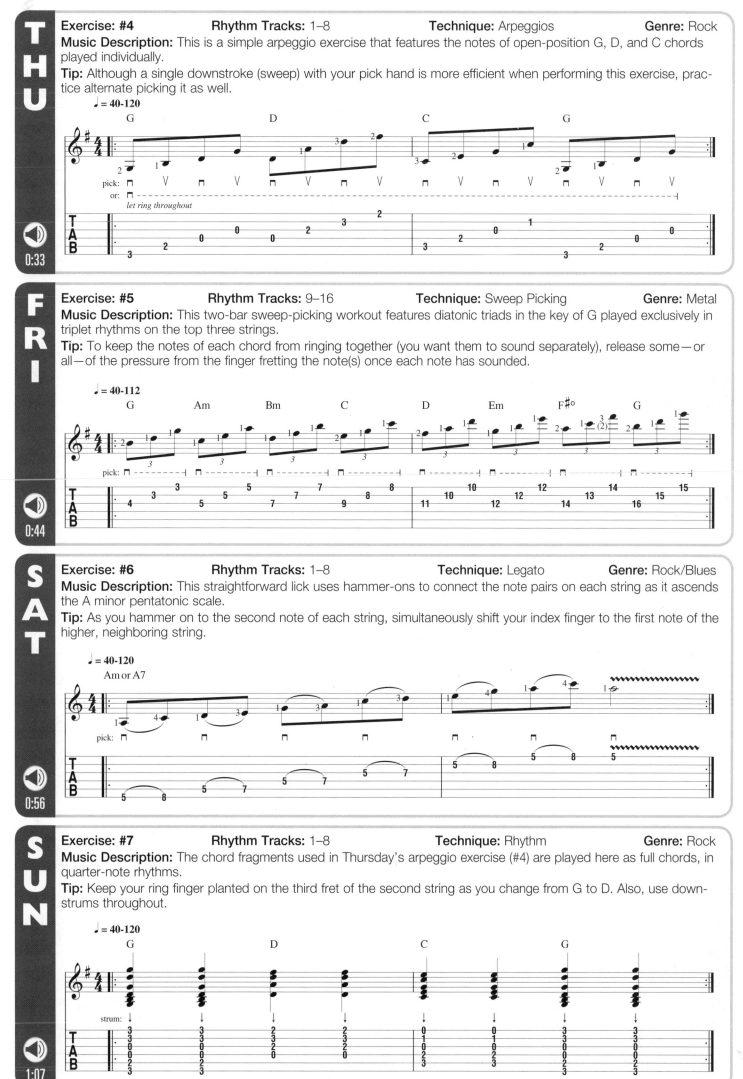

THU — 0:33

Exercise: #4   **Rhythm Tracks:** 1–8   **Technique:** Arpeggios   **Genre:** Rock

Music Description: This is a simple arpeggio exercise that features the notes of open-position G, D, and C chords played individually.

Tip: Although a single downstroke (sweep) with your pick hand is more efficient when performing this exercise, practice alternate picking it as well.

FRI — 0:44

Exercise: #5   **Rhythm Tracks:** 9–16   **Technique:** Sweep Picking   **Genre:** Metal

Music Description: This two-bar sweep-picking workout features diatonic triads in the key of G played exclusively in triplet rhythms on the top three strings.

Tip: To keep the notes of each chord from ringing together (you want them to sound separately), release some—or all—of the pressure from the finger fretting the note(s) once each note has sounded.

SAT — 0:56

Exercise: #6   **Rhythm Tracks:** 1–8   **Technique:** Legato   **Genre:** Rock/Blues

Music Description: This straightforward lick uses hammer-ons to connect the note pairs on each string as it ascends the A minor pentatonic scale.

Tip: As you hammer on to the second note of each string, simultaneously shift your index finger to the first note of the higher, neighboring string.

SUN — 1:07

Exercise: #7   **Rhythm Tracks:** 1–8   **Technique:** Rhythm   **Genre:** Rock

Music Description: The chord fragments used in Thursday's arpeggio exercise (#4) are played here as full chords, in quarter-note rhythms.

Tip: Keep your ring finger planted on the third fret of the second string as you change from G to D. Also, use downstrums throughout.

7

EXERCISE TRACK 2

MON

0:00

Exercise: #8   **Rhythm Tracks:** 9–16   **Technique:** Alternate Picking   **Genre:** Metal
Music Description: This lick is nearly identical to the one played last Monday (#1). The only variation is in the rhythm: Last week's lick was straight sixteenth notes, whereas this lick features a galloping, eighth-and-two-sixteenth-notes rhythm.
Tip: Use a strict down-down-up picking pattern throughout.

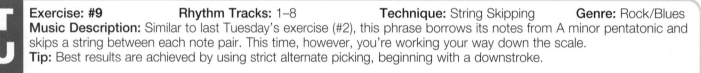

TUE

0:12

Exercise: #9   **Rhythm Tracks:** 1–8   **Technique:** String Skipping   **Genre:** Rock/Blues
Music Description: Similar to last Tuesday's exercise (#2), this phrase borrows its notes from A minor pentatonic and skips a string between each note pair. This time, however, you're working your way down the scale.
Tip: Best results are achieved by using strict alternate picking, beginning with a downstroke.

WED

0:23

Exercise: #10   **Rhythm Tracks:** 1–8   **Technique:** String Bending   **Genre:** Rock/Blues
Music Description: Releases have been added to the bends performed in last week's lick (#3).
Tip: Pay attention to this figure's rhythm, being careful not to rush each bend and release.

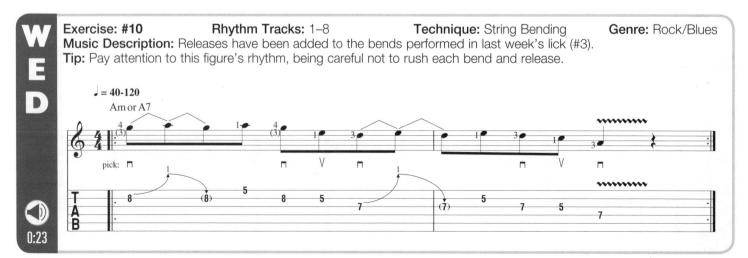

THU

Exercise: #11 **Rhythm Tracks:** 1–8 **Technique:** Arpeggios **Genre:** Rock

Music Description: This exercise is the descending version of last Thursday's arpeggio workout (#4).

Tip: A single upstroke (sweep) will work best when performing this exercise, but, like last week, alternate picking is encouraged as well.

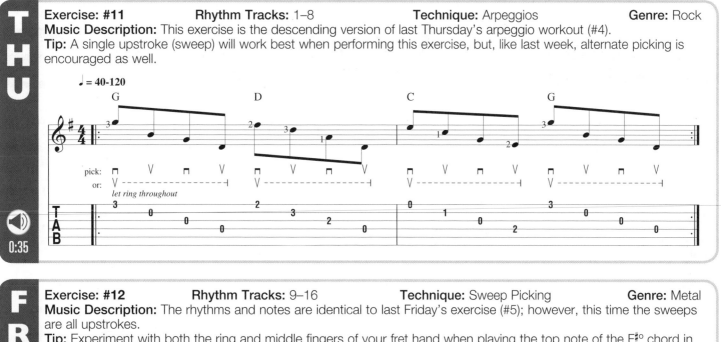

0:35

FRI

Exercise: #12 **Rhythm Tracks:** 9–16 **Technique:** Sweep Picking **Genre:** Metal

Music Description: The rhythms and notes are identical to last Friday's exercise (#5); however, this time the sweeps are all upstrokes.

Tip: Experiment with both the ring and middle fingers of your fret hand when playing the top note of the F#° chord in measure 2. Use whichever feels most comfortable.

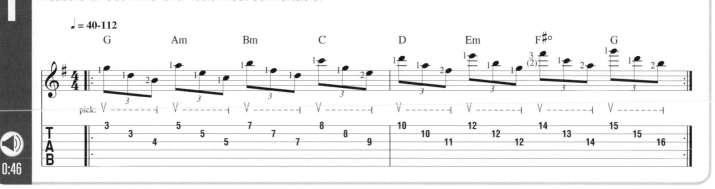

0:46

SAT

Exercise: #13 **Rhythm Tracks:** 1–8 **Technique:** Legato **Genre:** Rock/Blues

Music Description: This blues-rock lick is the descending, pull-offs version of last Saturday's exercise (#6).

Tip: To get the second note of each pair to sound as loud as the first, use a downward plucking motion when executing the pull-off.

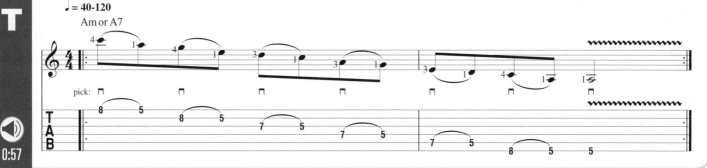

0:57

SUN

Exercise: #14 **Rhythm Tracks:** 1–8 **Technique:** Rhythm **Genre:** Rock

Music Description: This exercise features the same G–D–C–G chord changes as last Sunday's example (#7), only here the rhythm is straight eighth notes.

Tip: If you're having trouble making a smooth transition between chords, try lifting your hand off of the fretboard on the "and" of beats 2 and 4 of each measure. Don't worry about the open strings ringing; instead, focus on getting your fret hand to the next chord.

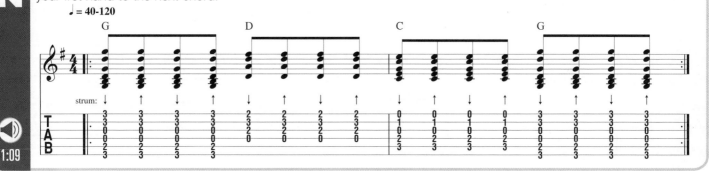

1:09

WEEK 3

EXERCISE TRACK 3

MON

Exercise: #15 **Rhythm Tracks:** 9–16 **Technique:** Alternate Picking **Genre:** Metal
Music Description: A continuation of Exercises #1 and #8 from the previous two Mondays, this exercise's only modification is its rhythm, which, here, is groupings of two sixteenth notes and an eighth note on each beat.
Tip: A down-up-down picking pattern on each beat is ideal for this example.

♩ = 40-112

0:00

TUE

Exercise: #16 **Rhythm Tracks:** 1–8 **Technique:** String Skipping **Genre:** Rock/Blues
Music Description: This lick is a variation of the ascending, play-two-notes-skip-one-string pattern (all within the framework of A minor pentatonic) from Exercise #2, only here the notes are played in reverse order.
Tip: This exercise is a bit more difficult for the fret hand to perform than the pervious two string-skipping figures, so take extra reps at slower tempos, if necessary, before moving on.

♩ = 40-120

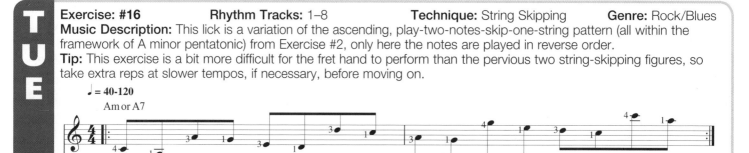

0:12

WED

Exercise: #17 **Rhythm Tracks:** 1–8 **Technique:** String Bending **Genre:** Rock/Blues
Music Description: This bending exercise is identical to the one from Week 1 (#3), except that the whole-step bends have been replaced with whole-step pre-bends and releases (the note is bent up one whole step before it's picked, and then released to it's original pitch).
Tip: Practice achieving proper intonation (hitting the target notes) on the pre-bends before attempting to play the entire lick.

♩ = 40-120

0:23

THU

0:35

Exercise: #18   **Rhythm Tracks:** 1–8   **Technique:** Arpeggios   **Genre:** Rock
Music Description: Portions of Exercises #4 and #11 have been combined to form this new arpeggio workout—various notes of open-position G, D, and C chords played in both ascending and descending fashion.
Tip: When playing the G chord, plant the ring finger of your fret hand on the third fret of the first string. Even though the note (G) is not played, it'll add stability to the chord voicing.

FRI

0:46

Exercise: #19   **Rhythm Tracks:** 9–16   **Technique:** Sweep Picking   **Genre:** Metal
Music Description: This is the same exercise as #5 from Week 1, only an extra chord tone (the 3rd for major chords; ♭3rd for minor and diminished chords) has been added to the top string.
Tip: Use the pinky of your fret hand and an upstroke with your pick hand to attack the last (highest) note of each four-note grouping.

SAT

0:58

Exercise: #20   **Rhythm Tracks:** 1–8   **Technique:** Legato   **Genre:** Rock/Blues
Music Description: Like the legato exercises from Weeks 1 and 2, the A minor pentatonic scale serves as the framework for this lick. This time, however, pull offs will be used while ascending the scale.
Tip: When executing the pull-offs, remember to pull down on the string to achieve adequate volume for the target note.

SUN

1:09

Exercise: #21   **Rhythm Tracks:** 1–8   **Technique:** Rhythm   **Genre:** Rock
Music Description: In the interest of giving last Sunday's G–D–C–D chord progression a bit more "forward motion," two sixteenth notes have been tacked on to the "and" of beats 2 and 4 of each measure.
Tip: To execute the sixteenth-note rhythms, follow the downstrums of beats 2 and 4 with quick down-upstrum patterns.

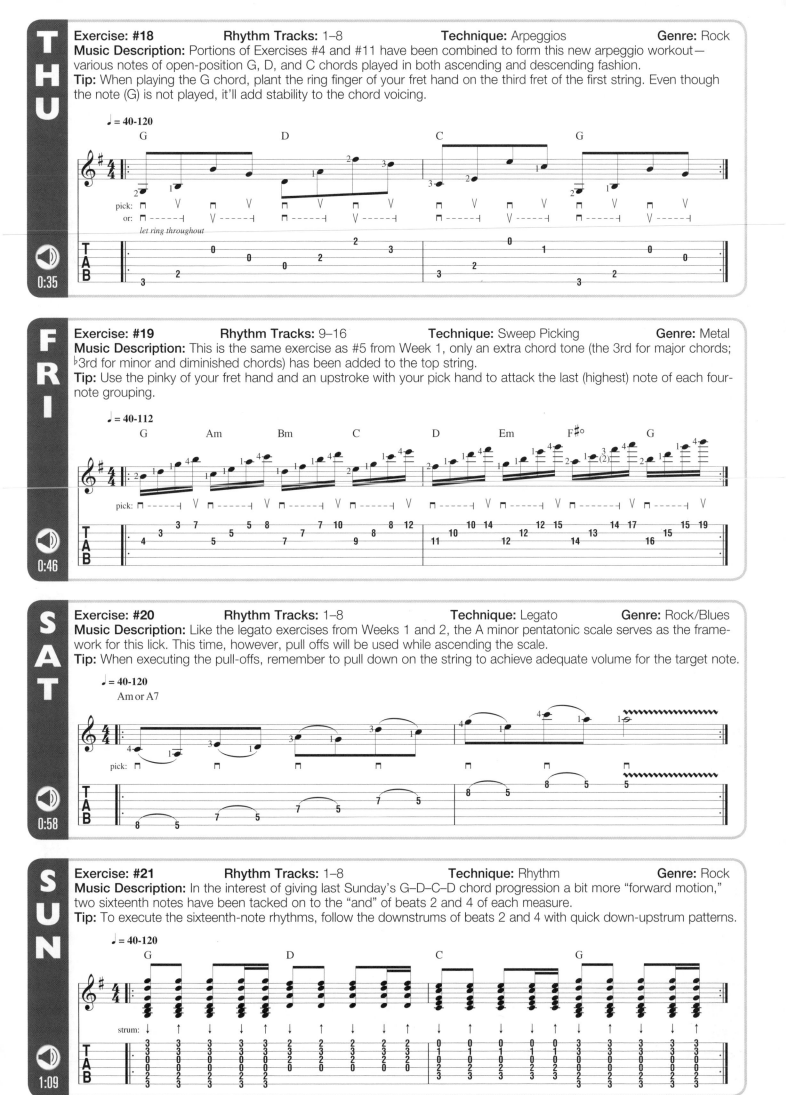

WEEK 4

EXERCISE TRACK 4

MON

Exercise: #22　　　**Rhythm Tracks:** 9–16　　　**Technique:** Alternate Picking　　　**Genre:** Metal

Music Description: This version of the E harmonic minor exercises of the past three weeks contains eighth-note triplet rhythms, which subdivide each beat into three equal parts.

Tip: Go slowly at first, and notice that, because of the triplets, the picking direction alternates between downstrokes and upstrokes on each downbeat.

0:00

TUE

Exercise: #23　　　**Rhythm Tracks:** 1–8　　　**Technique:** String Skipping　　　**Genre:** Rock/Blues

Music Description: Staying within the A minor pentatonic scale as in the previous string-skipping exercises, this phrase works its way down the scale, skipping a string between every other note pair.

Tip: Begin shifting your index finger to the next string as soon as your pinky or ring finger hits the second note on each string.

0:12

WED

Exercise: #24　　　**Rhythm Tracks:** 1–8　　　**Technique:** String Bending　　　**Genre:** Rock/Blues

Music Description: This exercise introduces two things: a whole-step bend on the first string performed with your pinky or ring finger and a half-step bend on the third string performed with your index finger.

Tip: That half-step bend is trickier than it seems; it's easy to fall flat or push it sharp. Play the target note, C♯, at the sixth fret of the third string to check your intonation.

0:23

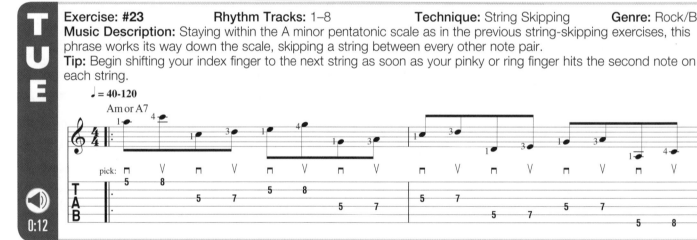

THU

🔊 0:34

Exercise: #25 **Rhythm Tracks:** 1–8 **Technique:** Arpeggios **Genre:** Rock

Music Description: This figure features the same G–D–C–G progression that has been used the previous three weeks; however, this time barre chords are utilized to voice the arpeggios.

Tip: Bar your index finger across all six strings when playing each arpeggio/chord.

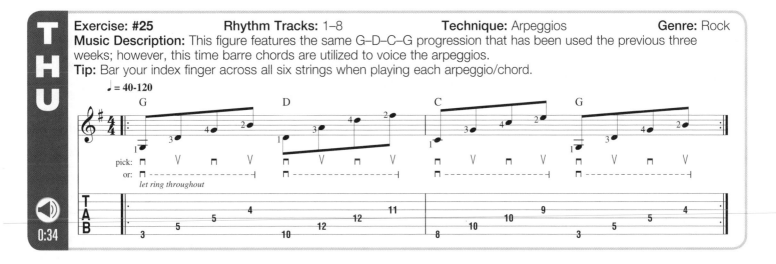

FRI

🔊 0:46

Exercise: #26 **Rhythm Tracks:** 9–16 **Technique:** Sweep Picking **Genre:** Metal

Music Description: This exercise is the descending version of last Friday's sweep-picking workout (#19).

Tip: The most efficient way to play each four-note grouping is by picking the first note with a downstroke and the last three notes with an upwards sweep.

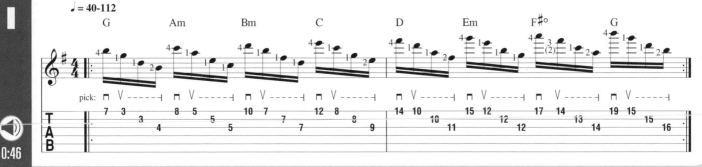

SAT

🔊 0:58

Exercise: #27 **Rhythm Tracks:** 1–8 **Technique:** Legato **Genre:** Rock/Blues

Music Description: Hammer-ons are used to connect the note pairs of each string while descending the A minor pentatonic scale in root position.

Tip: Be careful not to rush the hammer-ons; even eighth notes should be played through beat 2 of measure 2.

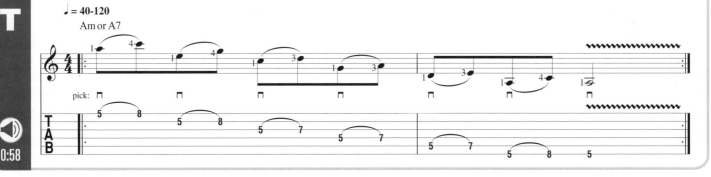

SUN

🔊 1:09

Exercise: #28 **Rhythm Tracks:** 1–8 **Technique:** Rhythm **Genre:** Rock

Music Description: The familiar G–D–C–G chord progression is the foundation for this exercise. The only difference between this example and last Sunday's exercise is the addition of two sixteenth notes on beats 1 and 3 of each measure.

Tip: Count each beat as "one-ee-and-uh, two-ee-and-uh" etc., and strum your pick hand accordingly; however, refrain from making contact with the strings on the "uh" of beats 1 and 3 and the "ee" of beats 2 and 4 of each measure.

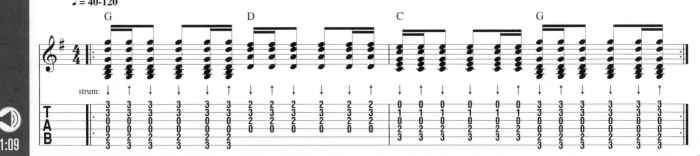

WEEK 5

EXERCISE TRACK 5

MON

0:00

Exercise: #29   **Rhythm Tracks:** 1–8   **Technique:** Alternate Picking   **Genre:** Rock/Blues
Music Description: This alternate-picking exercise runs straight up the A minor pentatonic scale, back-tracking only once (beat 3 of measure 2).
Tip: Once you're comfortable alternate picking the example starting with a downstroke, reverse your action and start with an upstroke.

TUE

0:11

Exercise: #30   **Rhythm Tracks:** 1–8   **Technique:** String Skipping   **Genre:** Rock/Blues
Music Description: The ubiquitous A minor pentatonic scale provides the framework for this next string-skipping exercise, a descending "sawtooth" line.
Tip: You might find it easier to perform this figure by starting with an upstroke in the first measure and reversing your picking direction in the second measure, starting with a downstroke.

WED

0:23

Exercise: #31   **Rhythm Tracks:** 1–8   **Technique:** String Bending   **Genre:** Rock/Blues
Music Description: Half-step bend-and-release moves on strings 1–3 are introduced in this next figure.
Tip: Like last Wednesday's lick (#24), be careful not to over-bend, causing the note to go sharp.

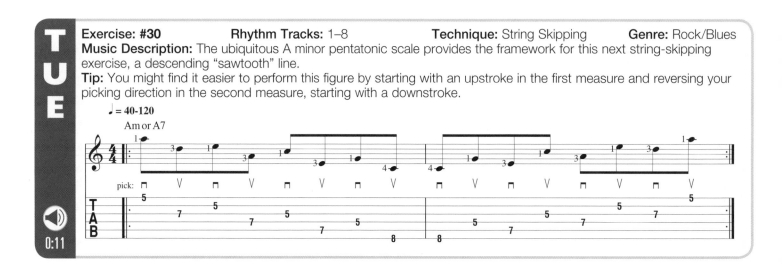

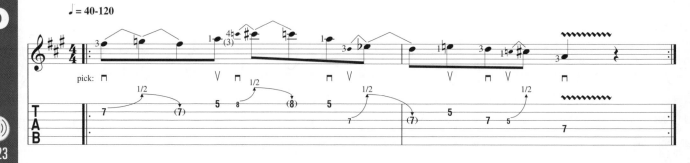

THU

Exercise: #32   **Rhythm Tracks:** 1–8   **Technique:** Arpeggios   **Genre:** Rock

Music Description: Don't let the tab staff fool you—these are the same barre chords from last Thursday's exercise (#25), only this time they're arpeggiated from high to low.

Tip: Like last week, bar all six strings with your index finger, forming the entire chord shape.

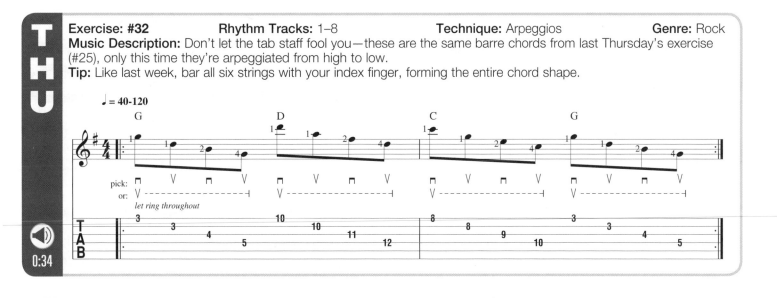

0:34

FRI

Exercise: #33   **Rhythm Tracks:** 9–16   **Technique:** Sweep Picking   **Genre:** Metal

Music Description: Except for the hammer-on, this figure is identical to Exercise #19 from Week 3. The hammer-on allows you to play all four notes with one pick motion.

Tip: Use a downward sweep to articulate the first three notes of the four-note grouping and then hammer onto the fourth note.

0:46

SAT

Exercise: #34   **Rhythm Tracks:** 1–8   **Technique:** Legato   **Genre:** Rock/Blues

Music Description: Featuring slides and hammer-ons, this lick climbs up the extended form of the A blues scale (A–C–D–E♭–E–G).

Tip: Pay close attention to the rhythm, because it features a mixture of quarter notes, eighth notes, and triplets.

0:57

SUN

Exercise: #35   **Rhythm Tracks:** 1–8   **Technique:** Rhythm   **Genre:** Rock

Music Description: In this example, the G–D–C–G chord progression from previous rhythm exercises is arranged in straight sixteenth notes throughout.

Tip: Remember to count: "one-ee-and-uh, two-ee-and-uh, three-ee-and-uh, four-ee-and-uh…"

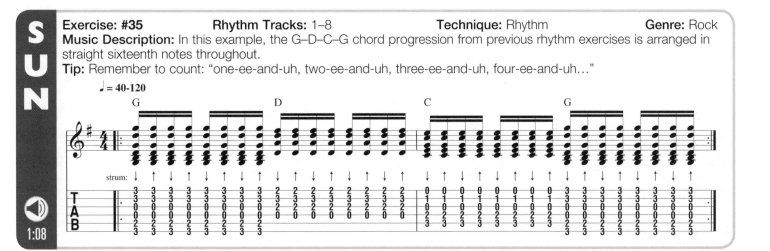

1:08

WEEK 6

EXERCISE TRACK 6

MON

Exercise: #36   **Rhythm Tracks:** 1–8   **Technique:** Alternate Picking   **Genre:** Rock/Blues
Music Description: This exercise features the A minor pentatonic scale arranged in a sequence of "ascending threes" (A–C–D, C–D–E, D–E–G, etc.).
Tip: Because of the triplet rhythm, the picking direction reverses itself on every beat so pay special attention to the picking prompt between the notation and tab staves.

0:00

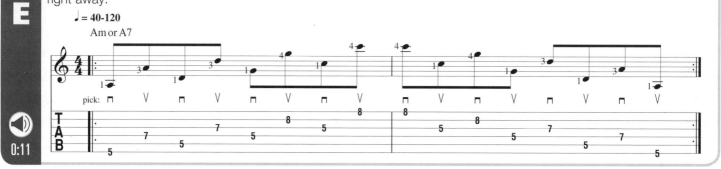

TUE

Exercise: #37   **Rhythm Tracks:** 1–8   **Technique:** String Skipping   **Genre:** Rock/Blues
Music Description: Octave jumps (A to A, C to C, D to D, etc.) within the A minor pentatonic form the basis of this exercise.
Tip: Two fret hand octave shapes (index/ring and index/pinky) are utilized throughout so become familiar with both right away.

0:11

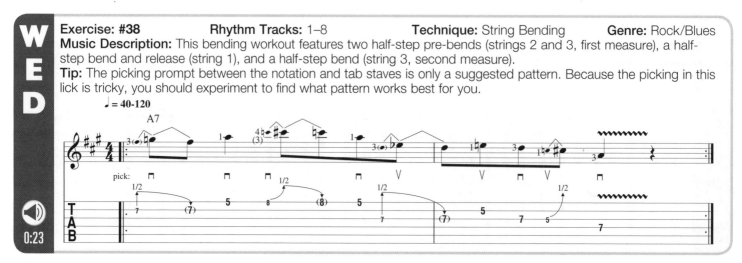

WED

Exercise: #38   **Rhythm Tracks:** 1–8   **Technique:** String Bending   **Genre:** Rock/Blues
Music Description: This bending workout features two half-step pre-bends (strings 2 and 3, first measure), a half-step bend and release (string 1), and a half-step bend (string 3, second measure).
Tip: The picking prompt between the notation and tab staves is only a suggested pattern. Because the picking in this lick is tricky, you should experiment to find what pattern works best for you.

0:23

THU

Exercise: #39 **Rhythm Tracks:** 1–8 **Technique:** Arpeggios **Genre:** Rock

Music Description: Like last Thursday's exercise (#32), G, D, and C barre chords are used once again. Here, a 6–5–2–3 string pattern is used to arpeggiate the six-string voicings.

Tip: Try using economy picking for this figure, whereby a single downstroke is used to play the bottom two notes and a single upstroke is used to play the top two notes.

0:34

FRI

Exercise: #40 **Rhythm Tracks:** 9–16 **Technique:** Sweep Picking **Genre:** Metal

Music Description: Unlike last Friday's lick (#33), in which a hammer-on allowed for four notes to be played with a single downwards sweep, this exercise demands a downpick and an upwards sweep, in addition to a pull-off. Still, it's much more efficient than picking each note individually.

Tip: Experiment with keeping your index finger barred across the top three strings as you move up the neck to play each shape.

0:45

SAT

Exercise: #41 **Rhythm Tracks:** 1–8 **Technique:** Legato **Genre:** Rock/Blues

Music Description: Like last Saturday's legato lick (#34), this phrase uses the extended A blues scale, only this time in descending fashion.

Tip: To achieve consistent volume levels for all of the notes, pull down on the string slightly when performing a pull-off.

0:57

SUN

Exercise: #42 **Rhythm Tracks:** 1–8 **Technique:** Rhythm **Genre:** Rock

Music Description: Embellishments, including hammer-ons, pull-offs, and additional notes, have been added to the same G–D–C–G chord progression that's featured in the rhythm exercises of the last several weeks.

Tip: When performing the hammer-on and pull-off arpeggiations, keep the preceding chord fretted (minus the fingers used for the embellishments) until the next chord change occurs.

1:08

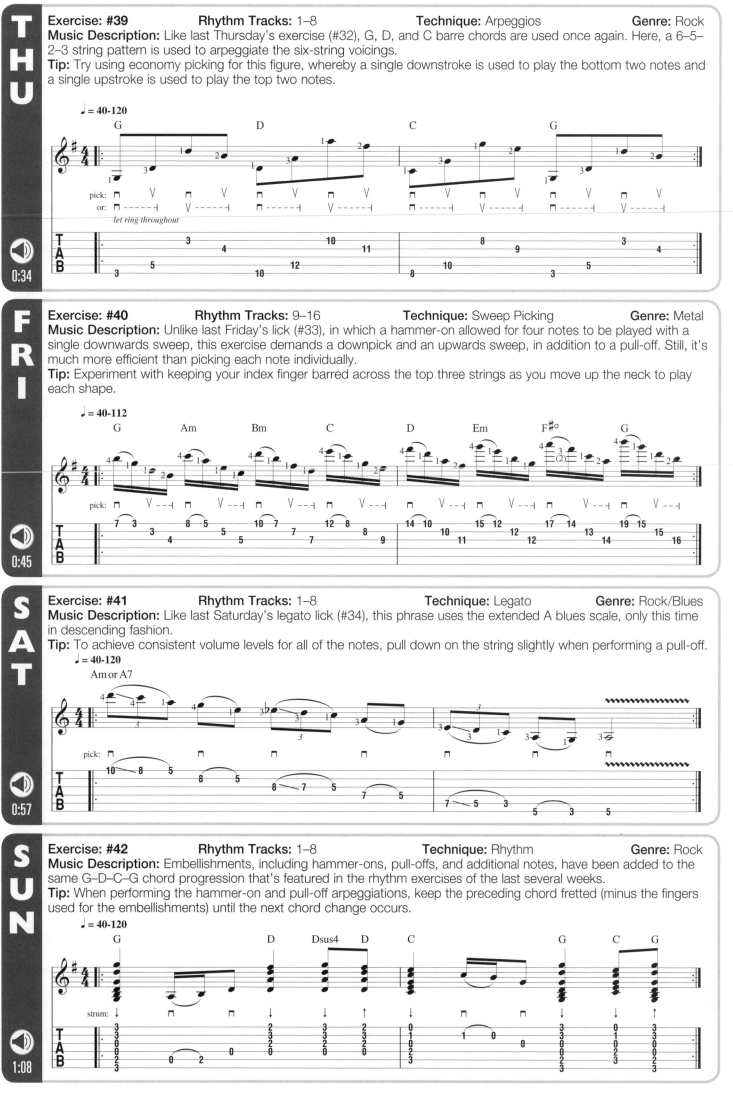

17

EXERCISE TRACK 7

MON

Exercise: #43 **Rhythm Tracks:** 1–8 **Technique:** Alternate Picking **Genre:** Rock/Blues

Music Description: This exercise takes last Monday's "ascending threes" sequence (#36) a step further, arranging the A minor pentatonic scale into "ascending fours" (A–C–D–E, C–D–E–G, D–E–G–A, etc.).

Tip: Unlike last week's triplet rhythm, this exercise is written in straight sixteenth notes so the picking direction is consistently downstrokes or upstrokes on each downbeat. Once you're comfortable starting the figure with a downstroke, try starting with an upstroke.

0:00

TUE

Exercise: #44 **Rhythm Tracks:** 17–24 **Technique:** String Skipping **Genre:** Blues

Music Description: The whole-step bend on the third string, followed by a string skip to the root note (A) on the first string, is a pentatonic move that was made popular by blues string-scorcher Stevie Ray Vaughan.

Tip: To facilitate a clean shift from eighth position (measure 1) to fifth position (measure 2), follow the suggested fingerings that are located below the tab staff.

0:11

WED

Exercise: #45 **Rhythm Tracks:** 17–24 **Technique:** String Bending **Genre:** Blues

Music Description: Quarter-step bends, also called "smears," are introduced in this exercise. Played on strings 1–3, the pitches are located halfway between the original fretted note and a half-step bend.

Tip: When performing a quarter-step bend, you're really not targeting a specific pitch; instead, aim for a pitch that sounds slightly out of tune.

0:19

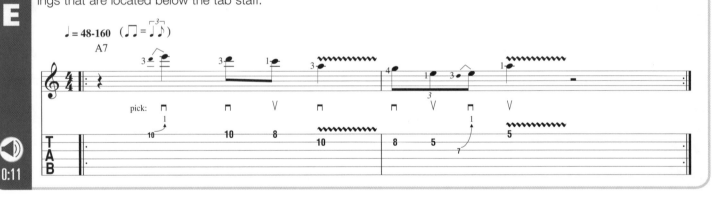

THU

Exercise: #46 **Rhythm Tracks:** 1–8 **Technique:** Arpeggios **Genre:** Rock

Music Description: Barre chords are the basis of this arpeggio workout, but here their roots are located on the fifth string rather than the sixth. The omnipresent G–D–C–G progression is utilized once again.

Tip: Because all of the chords are major, you're able to maintain the same voicing (index finger on string 5; ring-finger barre on strings 2–4) throughout.

♩ = 40-120

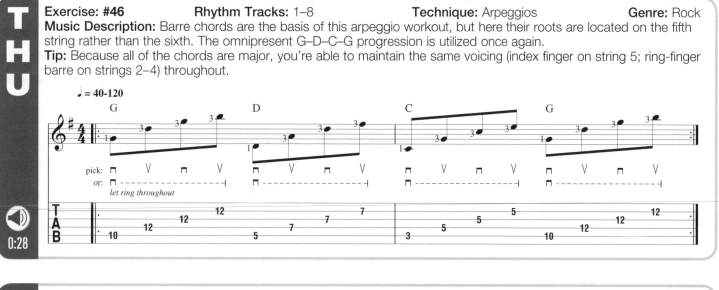

0:28

FRI

Exercise: #47 **Rhythm Tracks:** 9–16 **Technique:** Sweep Picking **Genre:** Metal

Music Description: Featuring sextuplet rhythms (two triplets per beat), this sweep-picking exercise, like the previous six, utilizes diatonic triads in the key of G.

Tip: Play the first triad (G) repeatedly, focusing on the strict picking pattern (downwards sweep followed by two upstokes), before moving on to the whole exercise.

♩ = 40-112

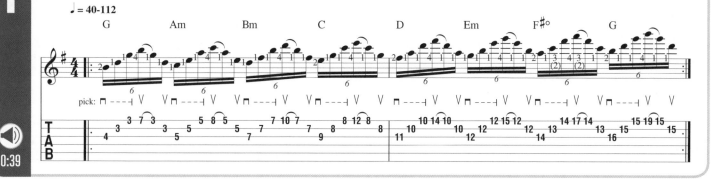

0:39

SAT

Exercise: #48 **Rhythm Tracks:** 1–8 **Technique:** Legato **Genre:** Rock/Blues

Music Description: Similar to the extended blues scale, the extended A minor pentatonic scale is the foundation of this legato lick. Highlights of this exercise include hammer-on/pull-off maneuvers on strings 1 and 6, and index-finger slides on strings 3 and 5.

Tip: Notice that the entire lick is played exclusively with the index and ring fingers of your fret hand.

♩ = 40-120

0:52

SUN

Exercise: #49 **Rhythm Tracks:** 1–8 **Technique:** Rhythm **Genre:** Rock

Music Description: This rhythm figure features ascending arpeggios that are voiced with basic open-position G, D, and C chords.

Tip: For efficiency's sake, use a single downstrum (i.e., sweep) for each chord shape.

♩ = 40-120

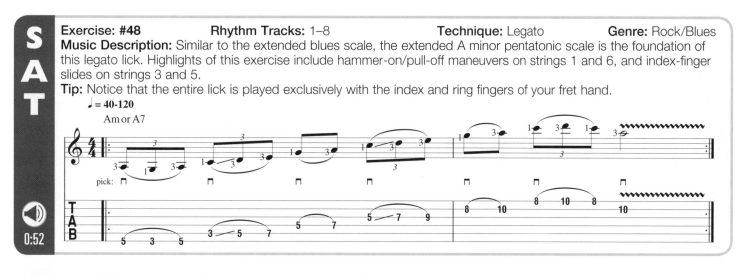

1:03

GUITAR
AEROBICS

WEEK 8

EXERCISE TRACK 8

MON

Exercise: #50　　　　**Rhythm Tracks:** 1–8　　　　**Technique:** Alternate Picking　　　　**Genre:** Rock/Blues
Music Description: The A minor pentatonic scale encompasses this alternate-picking exercise, which descends the scale, note for note, before reversing course on string 5.
Tip: Begin the exercise with an upstroke and end with a downstroke. Once you're comfortable with this pattern, start with a downstroke and end with an upstroke.

0:00

TUE

Exercise: #51　　　　**Rhythm Tracks:** 17–24　　　　**Technique:** String Skipping　　　　**Genre:** Blues
Music Description: This jagged A minor pentatonic line features multiple string skips throughout, both ascending and descending.
Tip: Bar your index finger across strings 1–3 at the fifth fret to minimize fret-hand movement.

0:10

WED

Exercise: #52　　　　**Rhythm Tracks:** 1–8　　　　**Technique:** String Bending　　　　**Genre:** Rock/Blues
Music Description: All of the bends you've learned up to this point (pre-bends, quarter-step, half-step, and whole-step) are arranged into a two-bar blues-rock example.
Tip: Watch out for the pre-bend on beat 3 of the first measure. This bend (and release) lasts a full beat, whereas the rest of the bends in the example are a half beat in length.

0:19

THU

Exercise: #53   **Rhythm Tracks:** 1–8   **Technique:** Arpeggios   **Genre:** Rock

Music Description: Last Thursday's arpeggiated G, D, and C barre chords, with the root on string 5, are used again in this workout, only in descending fashion.

Tip: Use the tip of your fret hand's index finger to mute string 6, so it doesn't ring sympathetically.

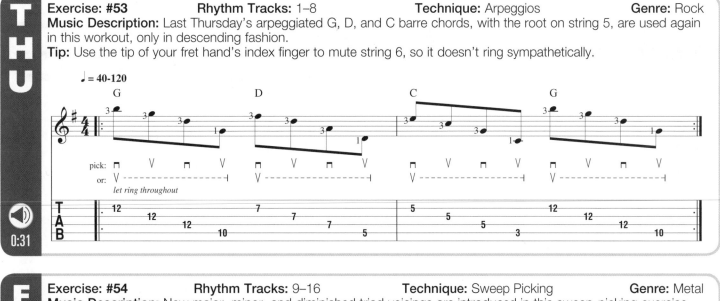

0:31

FRI

Exercise: #54   **Rhythm Tracks:** 9–16   **Technique:** Sweep Picking   **Genre:** Metal

Music Description: New major, minor, and diminished triad voicings are introduced in this sweep-picking exercise, which is arranged in triplets along the guitar's top three strings, in the key of D major.

Tip: For the minor triads, learn both fingerings; the alternate voicings will come in handy in subsequent exercises.

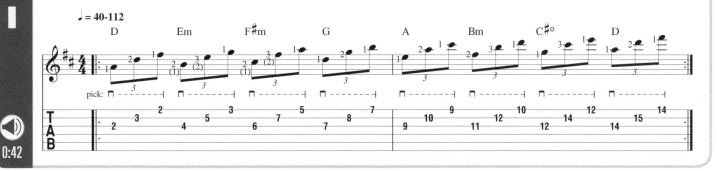

0:42

SAT

Exercise: #55   **Rhythm Tracks:** 1–8   **Technique:** Legato   **Genre:** Rock/Blues

Music Description: Featuring hammer-ons, pull-offs, and index-finger slides within the framework of the extended A minor pentatonic scale, this lick is the descending version of last week's legato exercise (#48).

Tip: Combine this exercise with last week's figure for an intense ascending/descending legato workout that covers a large chunk of fretboard real estate.

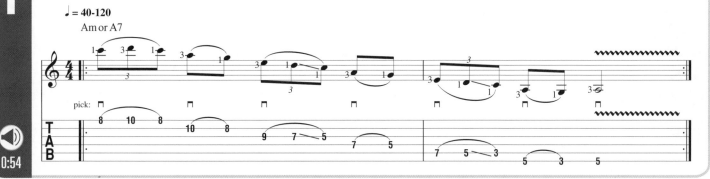

0:54

SUN

Exercise: #56   **Rhythm Tracks:** 1–8   **Technique:** Rhythm   **Genre:** Rock

Music Description: In this rhythm exercise, the arpeggios from Exercise 49 are restated; however, the sequence of the notes has been rearranged into a 6–2–3–4 string pattern.

Tip: In an effort to get to the next chord in rhythm, don't be afraid to lift you fingers off the fretboard on the last eighth note of each voicing. Although an open string may sound rather than a chord tone (in some cases, an open string will be a chord tone), few people will notice the difference. In fact, it's a trick practiced by virtually every guitarist on the planet.

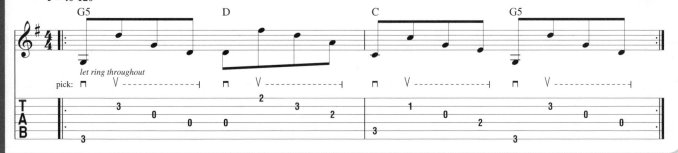

1:05

WEEK 9

EXERCISE TRACK 9

MON

Exercise: #57   **Rhythm Tracks:** 1–8   **Technique:** Alternate Picking   **Genre:** Rock/Blues
Music Description: The A minor pentatonic scale arranged in a sequence of "descending threes" forms the basis of this next exercise.
Tip: If you're having difficulty fretting the notes on the eighth fret with your pinky, use your ring finger instead.

0:00

TUE

Exercise: #58   **Rhythm Tracks:** 1–8   **Technique:** String Skipping   **Genre:** Rock/Blues
Music Description: This figure is similar to Exercise 2 of Week 1, only this time two strings are skipped between note pairs of the A minor pentatonic scale.
Tip: After you've played the first note of each note pair, simultaneously play the second note of the pair while you move your index finger into place for the first note of the next string.

0:11

WED

Exercise: #59   **Rhythm Tracks:** 1–8   **Technique:** String Bending   **Genre:** Rock/Blues
Music Description: This lick introduces two new bending techniques: playing fretted notes during a sustained bend (measure 1) and an oblique bend (measure 2). Like many of the previous bending exercises, this lick is performed in the root position of the A minor pentatonic scale.
Tip: Perform the seventh-fret bends with your ring finger, reinforcing it with your middle and index fingers.

0:25

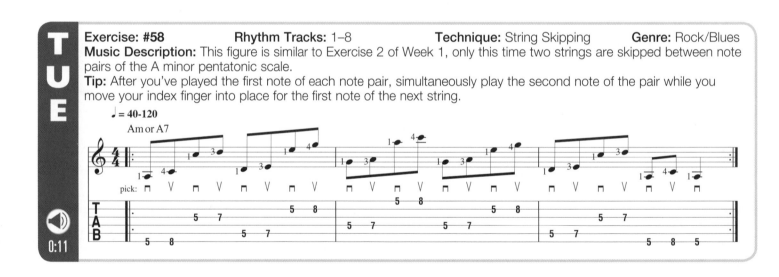

THU

Exercise: #60   **Rhythm Tracks:** 1–8   **Technique:** Arpeggios   **Genre:** Rock

Music Description: G, D, and C barre chords with fifth-string roots are arpeggiated in a 5–4–2–3 string sequence.

Tip: Once you're comfortable alternate picking this pattern, try a down-down-up-up economy picking pattern.

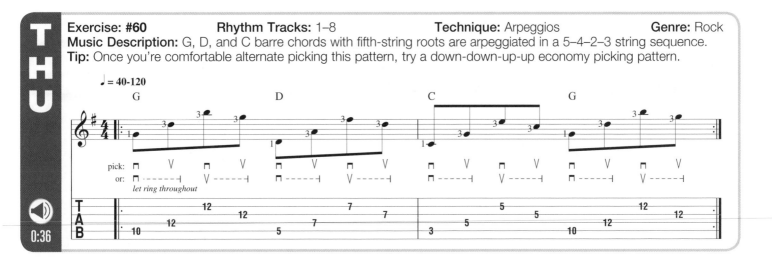

0:36

FRI

Exercise: #61   **Rhythm Tracks:** 9–16   **Technique:** Sweep Picking   **Genre:** Metal

Music Description: This figure is the descending version of last week's sweep-picking exercise (#54).

Tip: There are only three voicings used in this example. Once you have them under your fingers, it's only a matter of putting them in the proper sequence to play the entire exercise.

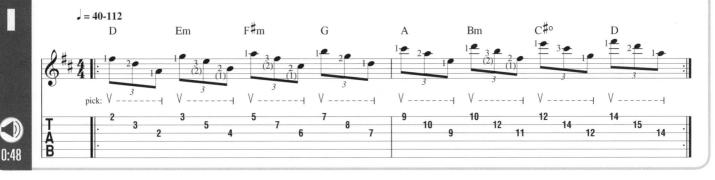

0:48

SAT

Exercise: #62   **Rhythm Tracks:** 1–8   **Technique:** Legato   **Genre:** Rock/Blues

Music Description: Featuring the E minor pentatonic scale, this exercise focuses on open-position hammer-ons and pull-offs. Play this lick over either an Em or E7 chord.

Tip: The fingerings notated below the tab staff are only a suggestion. You may also experiment with a combination of your middle and index fingers for the notes on frets 3 and 2, respectively.

1:00

SUN

Exercise: #63   **Rhythm Tracks:** 1–8   **Technique:** Rhythm   **Genre:** Rock

Music Description: In a consistent eighth-note rhythm, A minor, C major, G major, and E minor arpeggios, voiced as open-position chords, are played in an ascending/descending pattern that repeats on each new chord change.

Tip: Although the note is not played in this example, voice the E minor arpeggio as a standard open-position Em chord, whereby your fret hand's middle finger voices the note at fret 2 of the fifth string, and your middle finger voices the note at fret 2 of the fourth string.

1:11

WEEK 10

EXERCISE TRACK 10

MON

Exercise: #64   **Rhythm Tracks:** 1–8   **Technique:** Alternate Picking   **Genre:** Rock/Blues
Music Description: Here, the A minor pentatonic scale is arranged in "descending fours," landing on the sixth-string root note (A) on beat 4 of the second measure.
Tip: "Roll" your fret-hand index or ring fingers to play subsequent notes on the same fret of adjacent strings.

0:00

TUE

Exercise: #65   **Rhythm Tracks:** 1–8   **Technique:** String Skipping   **Genre:** Rock/Blues
Music Description: This exercise is the descending version of last Tuesday's A minor pentatonic string-skipping workout (#58).
Tip: Before playing through the entire figure, practice one string skip at a time (every two beats). Then combine all of beats, playing the whole exercise at the indicated tempos.

0:10

WED

Exercise: #66   **Rhythm Tracks:** 1–8   **Technique:** String Bending   **Genre:** Rock/Blues
Music Description: In this lick, yet another new bending technique is introduced: the whole-step unison bend. The term "unison bend" comes from the fact that the bent note is the same pitch as, or in unison with, the fretted note.
Tip: Performing the unison bend in measure 1 with your pinky will give you two fingers (ring and middle) with which to reinforce it.

0:25

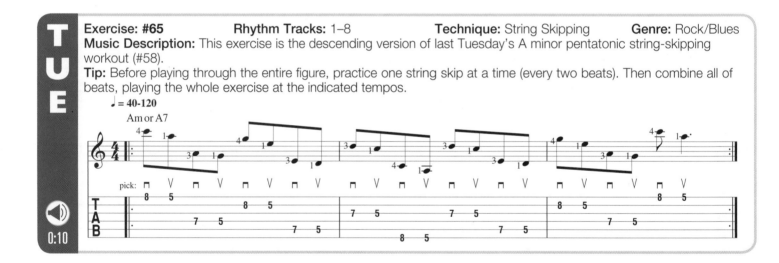

THU

Exercise: #67 **Rhythm Tracks:** 1–8 **Technique:** Arpeggios **Genre:** Rock

Music Description: Open-position Am, C, G, and Em chords are arpeggiated in an ascending/descending, one-chord-per-measure sequence. This is the same progression that's found in Metallica's "Fade to Black."

Tip: For the purpose of efficiency, try the alternate fingering shown in parentheses for the G chord.

0:36

FRI

Exercise: #68 **Rhythm Tracks:** 9–16 **Technique:** Sweep Picking **Genre:** Metal

Music Description: In this example, a continuation of last week's exercise (#61), an additional 5th of each triad (A for D major, B for E minor, C♯ for F♯ minor, etc.) has been added to the top string.

Tip: After employing a single downwards sweep for the first three notes, use an upstroke for the last note of each four-note grouping.

0:54

SAT

Exercise: #69 **Rhythm Tracks:** 1–8 **Technique:** Legato **Genre:** Rock/Blues

Music Description: A highlight of this open-position pull-off exercise, featuring the E minor pentatonic scale, is the triplet-based legato slides that occur on string 3—a favorite move of Jimi Hendrix and Stevie Ray Vaughan.

Tip: Follow the suggested fingerings that are notated below the tab staff. By starting the phrase with your ring finger, you'll free your middle and index fingers to perform the slides that appear on beats 3 and 4.

1:06

SUN

Exercise: #70 **Rhythm Tracks:** 1–8 **Technique:** Rhythm **Genre:** Rock

Music Description: The A minor, C major, G major, and E minor arpeggios from last Sunday (#63) have been retained for this example, although the rhythms are slightly different, and a new technique—hammer-ons—has been added to the mix.

Tip: Don't let the picking prompt, which is noted between staves, intimidate you. A down-sweep is still employed for the arpeggios' ascent and an up-sweep is used for their descent. The hammer-ons, however, break up the continuous motion of some of the sweeps.

1:17

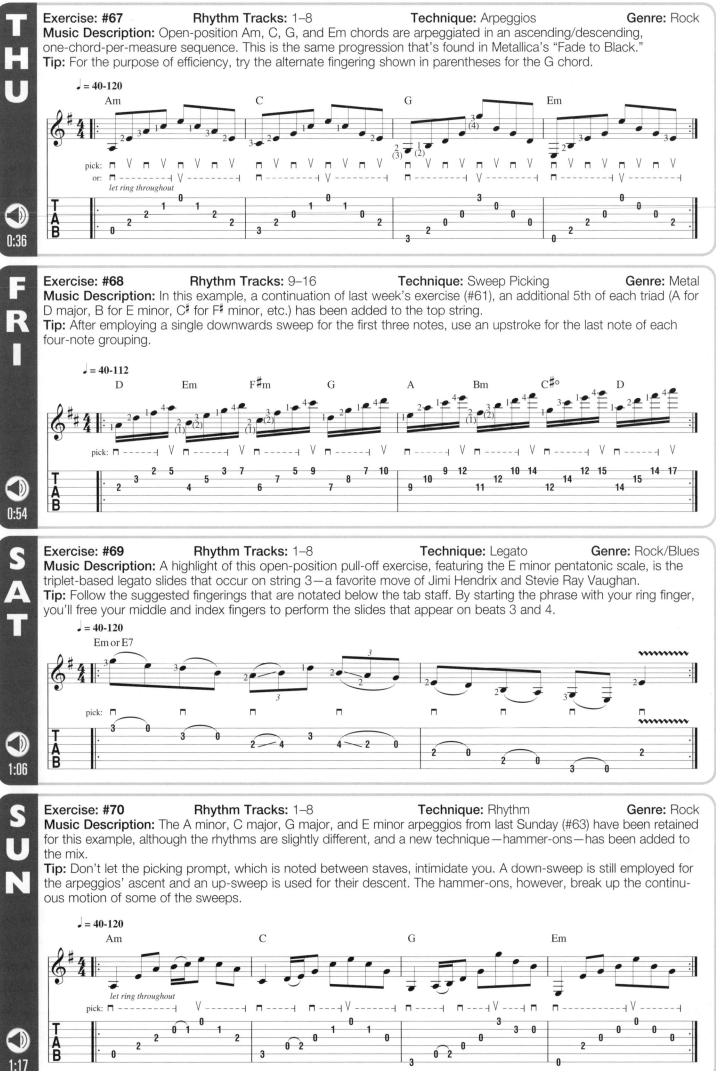

EXERCISE TRACK 11

MON

Exercise: #71 **Rhythm Tracks:** 17–24 **Technique:** Alternate Picking **Genre:** Blues
Music Description: This triplet-based alternate-picking workout incorporates bends to form an applicable A minor pentatonic blues lick.
Tip: Follow the picking directions notated between the tab and notation staves to facilitate the bends, which must be performed quickly to maintain the strict triplet rhythms.

♩ = 40-120

0:00

TUE

Exercise: #72 **Rhythm Tracks:** 1–8 **Technique:** String Skipping **Genre:** Rock/Blues
Music Description: This exercise is similar to the ascending A minor pentatonic string-skipping workout from Exercise 58, only the order of the note pairs on each string are reversed.
Tip: Although the picking prompt indicates a downstroke should begin the exercise, experiment with using an upstroke to start the figure. Practice both picking patterns many times at the tempos indicated.

♩ = 40-120

0:11

WED

Exercise: #73 **Rhythm Tracks:** 1–8 **Technique:** String Bending **Genre:** Rock
Music Description: Unison bends are performed exclusively along strings 1 and 2, ascending the A natural minor scale (A–B–C–D–E–F–G).
Tip: Make note (no pun intended) of the pitches on string 1 and use them to visually target each position shift.

♩ = 40-120

0:25

THU

Exercise: #74   **Rhythm Tracks:** 1–8   **Technique:** Arpeggios   **Genre:** Rock

Music Description: This arpeggio figure borrows the Am–C–G–Em progression from Exercise 67; however, here sixth-string-rooted barre chords are utilized rather than open chords.

Tip: To change from the Am barre-chord voicing to the C major voicing, simply add your middle finger to string 3; remove it to change from G to Em.

0:37

FRI

Exercise: #75   **Rhythm Tracks:** 9–16   **Technique:** Sweep Picking   **Genre:** Metal

Music Description: The sweep-picked triads from last week (#68) are arranged here in descending fashion.

Tip: After playing the first note of each four-note grouping (one beat) with a downstroke, use a single upwards sweep to articulate the remaining three notes.

0:55

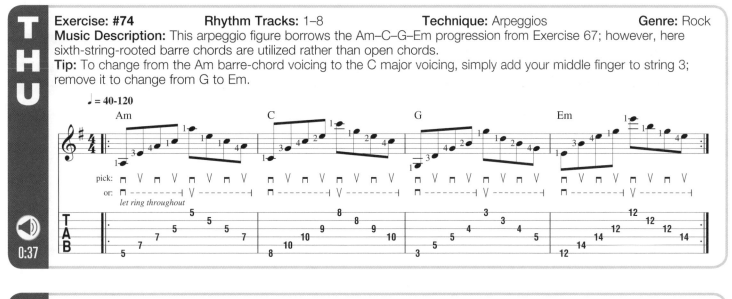
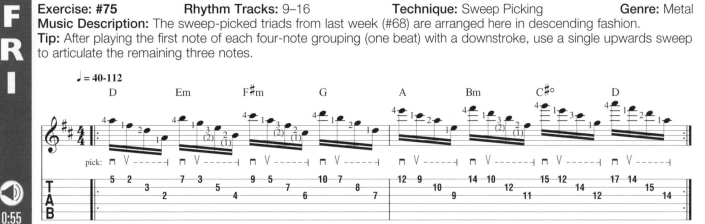

SAT

Exercise: #76   **Rhythm Tracks:** 1–8   **Technique:** Legato   **Genre:** Rock/Blues

Music Description: Based in the E blues scale, this open-position legato line features alternating three-note and two-note pull-offs as it descends the strings.

Tip: Use a combination of right- and left-hand muting to prevent unwanted string noise, especially from previously played open strings.

1:07

SUN

Exercise: #77   **Rhythm Tracks:** 1–8   **Technique:** Rhythm   **Genre:** Rock

Music Description: Similar to last Sunday's rhythm exercise, Am, C, G, and Em arpeggios are arranged in an ascending/descending pattern; however, in lieu of hammer-ons, pull-offs are added to three of the four arpeggios.

Tip: The most efficient way to voice the G major arpeggio is to move your fret hand's ring finger from fret 3 of the fifth string (its location for the C chord/arpeggio) to fret 3 of the sixth string. That way, you can use your pinky finger, similar to the Am and C arpeggios, to perform the pull-off on string 2.

1:18

WEEK 12

EXERCISE TRACK 12

MON

Exercise: #78 **Rhythm Tracks:** 17–24 **Technique:** Alternate Picking **Genre:** Blues
Music Description: This lick opens with an "ascending threes" sequence of the A minor pentatonic scale, features whole- and quarter-step bends, and resolves to the root note (A) on the fourth string.
Tip: Review Exercise 36 from Week 6 (ascending threes) before tackling this exercise.

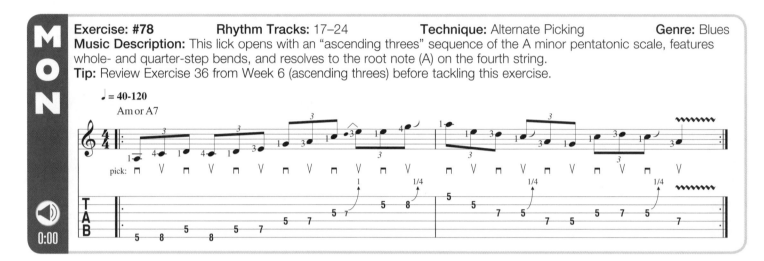

0:00

TUE

Exercise: #79 **Rhythm Tracks:** 1–8 **Technique:** String Skipping **Genre:** Rock/Blues
Music Description: Like the licks from the previous three Tuesdays (#58, #65, and #72), this exercise, the final of its kind, features two-string skips arranged within the confines of the A minor pentatonic scale.
Tip: Use your pinky (instead of your ring finger) to play the notes at the eighth fret of strings 1, 2 and 6.

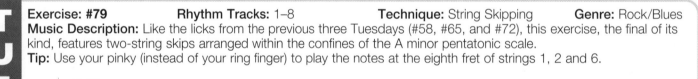

0:11

WED

Exercise: #80 **Rhythm Tracks:** 1–8 **Technique:** String Bending **Genre:** Rock
Music Description: Playing the A natural minor scale starting on the fifth degree, E, yields the E Phrygian mode, which provides the notes for this unison-bend exercise played exclusively on strings 2 and 3.
Tip: Listen closely so that each bend arrives at its target pitch (unison) before moving on to the next bend.

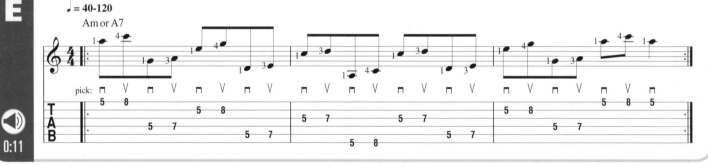

0:25

Exercise: #81   **Rhythm Tracks:** 1–8   **Technique:** Arpeggios   **Genre:** Rock

Music Description: Fifth-string-rooted barre chords, utilizing the Am–C–G–Em progression of the previous two Thursdays, form the foundation for this arpeggio exercise.

Tip: To articulate the highest note of each major barre-chord arpeggio, you may find it necessary to briefly lift your ring finger off of the fretboard, reapplying it for the arpeggio's descent.

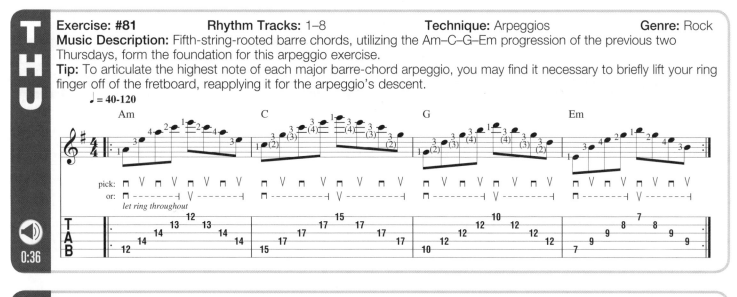

0:36

Exercise: #82   **Rhythm Tracks:** 9–16   **Technique:** Sweep Picking   **Genre:** Metal

Music Description: Note for note, this figure is identical to the one from Exercise 68 except that, here, a hammer-on is employed to connect the notes on string 1 for each triad.

Tip: After sweep picking the first three notes of each chord, hammer on your pinky finger to articulate the fourth, and final, note of each grouping.

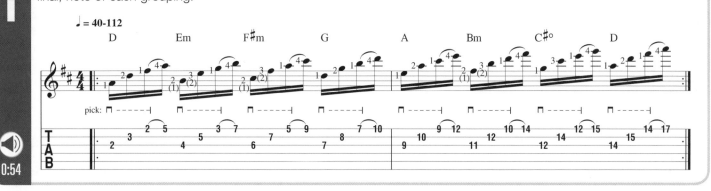

0:54

Exercise: #83   **Rhythm Tracks:** 1–8   **Technique:** Legato   **Genre:** Rock/Blues

Music Description: Similar to last Saturday's legato exercise (#76), this phrase also features the E blues scale; however, here the notes ascend the strings via alternating two-note and three-note hammer-ons.

Tip: Try mixing and matching portions of this figure with last week's example, improvising your own ascending/descending open-position legato lines.

1:06

Exercise: #84   **Rhythm Tracks:** 1–8   **Technique:** Rhythm   **Genre:** Rock

Music Description: In this rhythm workout, Am, C, G, and Em arpeggios are arranged in a distinct pattern called "Travis picking," which got its name from the country picker who popularized the technique, Merle Travis.

Tip: If you choose to fingerpick this pattern, notice that your pick hand's thumb plays the notes on the strong beats (the bass notes) and your index, middle, and ring fingers alternate between the notes on the weak beats.

1:17

EXERCISE TRACK 13

MON

Exercise: #85   **Rhythm Tracks:** 1–8   **Technique:** Alternate Picking   **Genre:** Rock

Music Description: This basic two-bar, two-chord (C–Am) figure, featuring ascending and descending arpeggios, is designed to enhance your adjacent-string alternate-picking chops.

Tip: Fight your inclination to use a single downstrum and upstrum to play the ascending and descending arpeggios, respectively.

TUE

Exercise: #86   **Rhythm Tracks:** 1–8   **Technique:** String Skipping   **Genre:** Rock/Blues

Music Description: Some of the string skips that you've learned up to this point are featured in this applicable blues lick in A. (Specifically, beginning on the "and" of beat 3 of measure 1, and the last two notes of measure 2.)

Tip: Use the picking prompt and suggested fret-hand fingerings for advice on how to perform this lick most efficiently.

WED

Exercise: #87   **Rhythm Tracks:** 1–8   **Technique:** String Bending   **Genre:** Rock

Music Description: Unison bends are paired with unison pre-bends in this exercise, which descends the A natural minor scale, note for note, as it travels down strings 1 and 2.

Tip: After you perform the unison bend, be sure to maintain proper tension on string 2, or the pre-bend will be either sharp or flat.

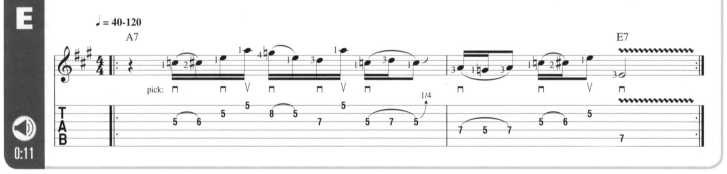

THU

Exercise: #88   **Rhythm Tracks:** 1–8   **Technique:** Arpeggios   **Genre:** Rock

Music Description: This arpeggio figure combines the open-position chords and barre chords of the exercises from the previous three Thursdays (#67, #74, and #81), in the familiar Am–C–G–Em progression.

Tip: When repeating the phrase, don't worry about having to quickly move from seventh position to open position, because the first note of the first measure is an open string, which allows for an easy transition.

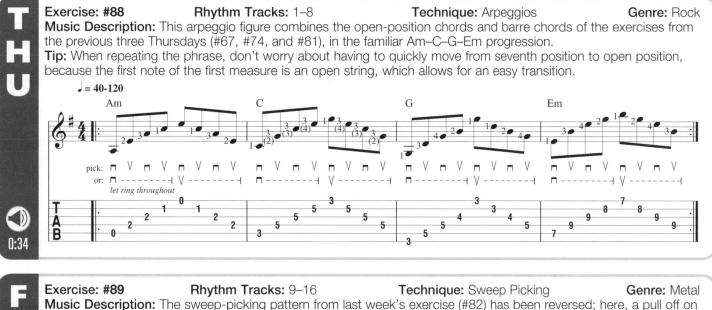

0:34

FRI

Exercise: #89   **Rhythm Tracks:** 9–16   **Technique:** Sweep Picking   **Genre:** Metal

Music Description: The sweep-picking pattern from last week's exercise (#82) has been reversed; here, a pull off on the top string is followed by an upwards sweep of strings 2 and 3.

Tip: Unlike last week's figure, here you are sweeping two strings instead of three—the notes on string 1 are articulated with a downstroke and a pull off.

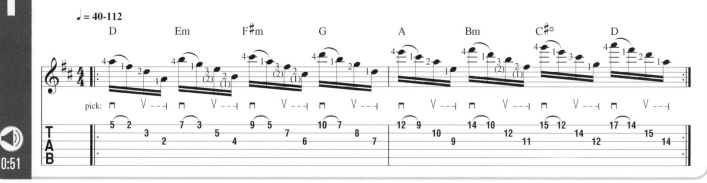

0:51

SAT

Exercise: #90   **Rhythm Tracks:** 1–8   **Technique:** Legato   **Genre:** Rock/Blues

Music Description: Hammer-ons and pull-offs are used to ascend and descend this E blues-scale lick. The open B and high E strings are played in concert to cap the phrase and reinforce the key center (E).

Tip: The quick hammer/pull found on the "and" of beat 2 of the second measure is a sixteenth-note triplet (three notes are crammed into a half beat). Spend some extra time getting that rhythm down before attempting to play the entire lick.

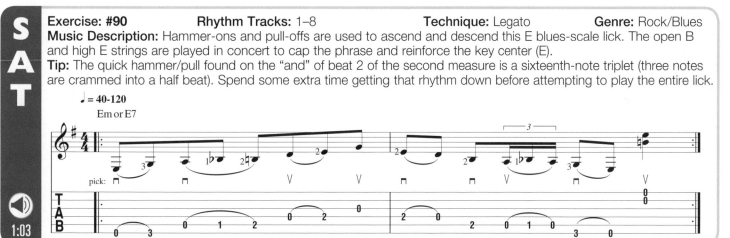

1:03

SUN

Exercise: #91   **Rhythm Tracks:** 1–8   **Technique:** Rhythm   **Genre:** Rock

Music Description: This finger-picking figure takes last Sunday's exercise (#84) a few steps further by first adding an extra chord tone to beat 1 of each measure, modifying the picking pattern slightly, and then including passing chords (G/B, D, or D/F#) on beat 4 of every measure of the Am–C–G–Em progression.

Tip: Once you have this pattern under your fingers, try adding some of the embellishments that were presented in previous rhythm exercises, such as hammer-ons and pull-offs, to the proceedings.

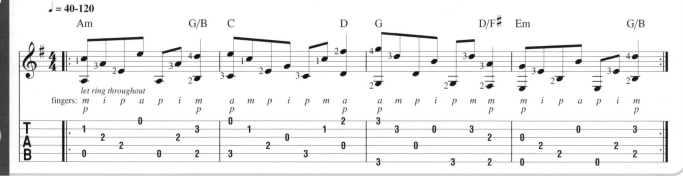

1:14

EXERCISE TRACK 14

MON

Exercise: #92 **Rhythm Tracks:** 1–8 **Technique:** Alternate Picking **Genre:** Rock
Music Description: An extension of last week's exercise (#85), this figure focuses on using alternate picking to articulate ascending arpeggios that alternate between starting on the fifth and fourth strings.
Tip: Keep both chords (C and Am) fingered for the entire measure, lifting your fret-hand fingers only to switch voicings.

0:00

TUE

Exercise: #93 **Rhythm Tracks:** 1–8 **Technique:** String Skipping **Genre:** Rock/Blues
Music Description: This blues turnaround lick in A features one- and two-string skips in measure 1, and one-string skips in measure 2.
Tip: In measure 1, keeping your index finger barred across strings 1–3 will facilitate the fifth-fret string skips.

0:11

WED

Exercise: #94 **Rhythm Tracks:** 1–8 **Technique:** String Bending **Genre:** Rock
Music Description: This exercise is similar to last Wednesday's workout (#87), only here the bends have been moved to strings 2 and 3, and the A natural minor scale starts on its fifth degree, E, which can also be thought of as the E Phrygian mode.
Tip: For better note clarity, pick this exercise with downstrokes exclusively.

0:23

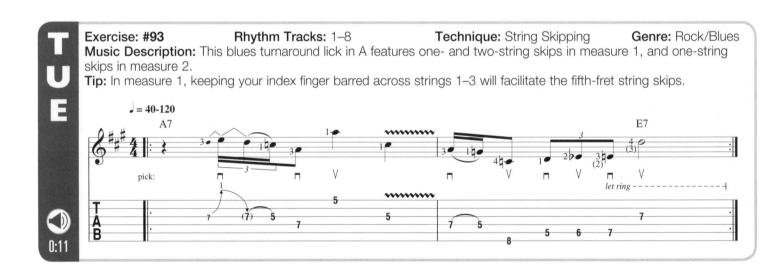

32

THU

🔊 0:34

Exercise: #95   **Rhythm Tracks:** 1–8   **Technique:** Arpeggios   **Genre:** Rock

Music Description: In this arpeggio workout, the chord voicings from last Thursday's exercise (#88) are used once again, only this time just the top three notes are played.

Tip: To voice these chords, you can choose one of two options: use the full open chords and barre chords from Exercise 88, or use the fingerings provided here, below the tab staff.

FRI

🔊 0:45

Exercise: #96   **Rhythm Tracks:** 9–16   **Technique:** Sweep Picking   **Genre:** Metal

Music Description: Elements from the previous six sweep-picking exercises are incorporated into this sextuplet figure, including triads in the key of D, downward sweeps, and pull-offs.

Tip: While you shift positions, use your fret-hand index finger as a guide, moving it along string 3 from fret to fret.

SAT

🔊 0:57

Exercise: #97   **Rhythm Tracks:** 1–8   **Technique:** Legato   **Genre:** Rock/Blues

Music Description: Highlights of this open-position E blues-scale lick include slides on string 2, both of which incorporate the unison open E string, and a sixteenth-note triplet pull-off on the "and" of beat 4 of the first measure.

Tip: To execute the unison slide at the end of the lick, your ring finger needs enough arch so as to avoid muting the open high E string.

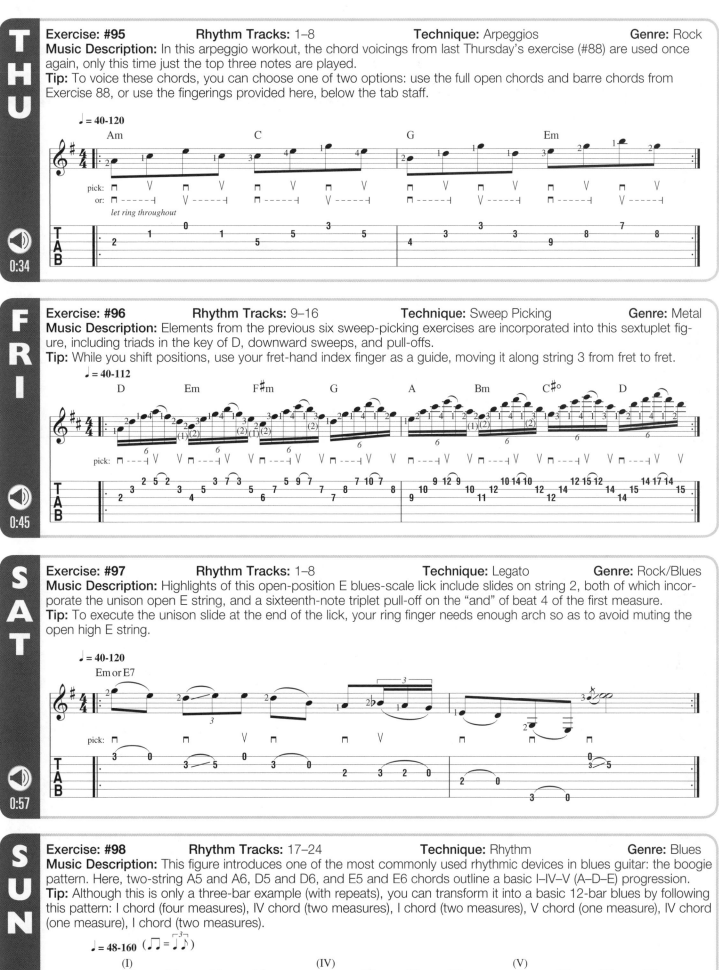

SUN

🔊 1:08

Exercise: #98   **Rhythm Tracks:** 17–24   **Technique:** Rhythm   **Genre:** Blues

Music Description: This figure introduces one of the most commonly used rhythmic devices in blues guitar: the boogie pattern. Here, two-string A5 and A6, D5 and D6, and E5 and E6 chords outline a basic I–IV–V (A–D–E) progression.

Tip: Although this is only a three-bar example (with repeats), you can transform it into a basic 12-bar blues by following this pattern: I chord (four measures), IV chord (two measures), I chord (two measures), V chord (one measure), IV chord (one measure), I chord (two measures).

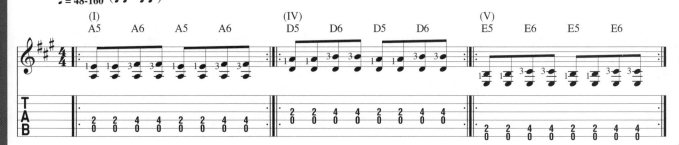

WEEK 15

EXERCISE TRACK 15

MON

Exercise: #99 **Rhythm Tracks:** 1–8 **Technique:** Alternate Picking **Genre:** Rock
Music Description: In addition to the inherent challenges presented when alternate picking notes on adjacent strings, this C–Am arpeggio figure features the difficult task of skipping over strings 2 and 4 as well.
Tip: Isolate the C arpeggio and practice the picking pattern and string jumps, and then incorporate the Am arpeggio into the full exercise.

♩ = 40-120

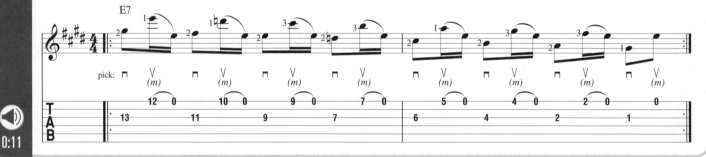

0:00

TUE

Exercise: #100 **Rhythm Tracks:** 33–40 **Technique:** String Skipping **Genre:** Country
Music Description: Featuring major- and minor-sixth intervals from the E Mixolydian mode along strings 1 and 3 exclusively, this country pull-off lick provides great practice for rapidly skipping over a single string multiple times.
Tip: You can pick this lick two ways: with either alternate picking or *hybrid* picking, which is a combination of a down-stroke with your pick and an upstroke with your middle finger.

♩ = 60-184

0:11

WED

Exercise: #101 **Rhythm Tracks:** 1–8 **Technique:** String Bending **Genre:** Rock/Blues
Music Description: *Compound bends* are introduced in this lick, which is rooted in the A minor pentatonic scale (with an added F♯). Compound bends are most often referred to as any bends that exceed a whole step; in this case, 1½- and two-step bends.
Tip: For this lick, you'll want to use a guitar with light strings, preferably .009s or .010s. Also, be sure to use your index and middle fingers to reinforce the bend.

♩ = 40-120

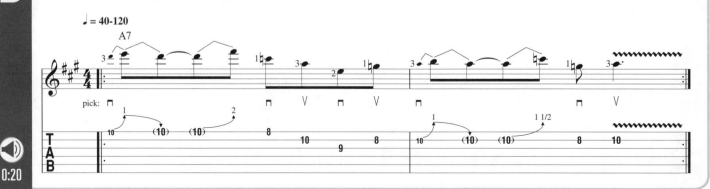

0:20

THU

0:31

Exercise: #102 **Rhythm Tracks:** 1–8 **Technique:** Arpeggios **Genre:** Rock

Music Description: This figure is nearly identical to last Thursday's arpeggio exercise (#95); the only differences are that the voicings have been shifted down to strings 2–4, the notes of the G chord are slightly rearranged, and the last chord, Em, has been transposed to a lower octave.

Tip: While you're playing the open strings of the Em arpeggio, shift your fret hand up to fifth position so that it's in place for the Am arpeggio, on the repeat.

FRI

0:42

Exercise: #103 **Rhythm Tracks:** 9–16 **Technique:** Sweep Picking **Genre:** Metal

Music Description: In this next figure, three new voicings of major, minor, and diminished triads are arranged in the key of C, in stepwise fashion, along strings 1–3.

Tip: To sweep pick the major triads, use your fret hand's ring finger to bar across strings 3 and 2.

SAT

0:54

Exercise: #104 **Rhythm Tracks:** 1–8 **Technique:** Legato **Genre:** Rock/Blues

Music Description: Reminiscent of Eric Clapton's turnaround lick in Cream's "Crossroads," this next legato line, based predominantly in A minor pentatonic (with an added major 3rd, C♯), features an assortment of hammer-ons and pull-offs on strings 2–4.

Tip: There is no rhythmic value assigned to the hammer-on that occurs on beat 2 of the second measure. To perform it properly, simply hammer your finger down onto string 3 as quickly as possible.

SUN

1:05

Exercise: #105 **Rhythm Tracks:** 17–24 **Technique:** Rhythm **Genre:** Blues

Music Description: A variation of the rhythm figure from last Sunday (#98), this boogie pattern, rooted in the key of A, adds dominant seventh chords to the I–IV–V (A–D–E) progression.

Tip: Some guitarists prefer to slide their ringer finger up one fret to play the dominant chords (A7, D7, and E7) on beat 3 of each measure. That's perfectly acceptable but, for efficiency's sake, I suggest that you instead use your pinky.

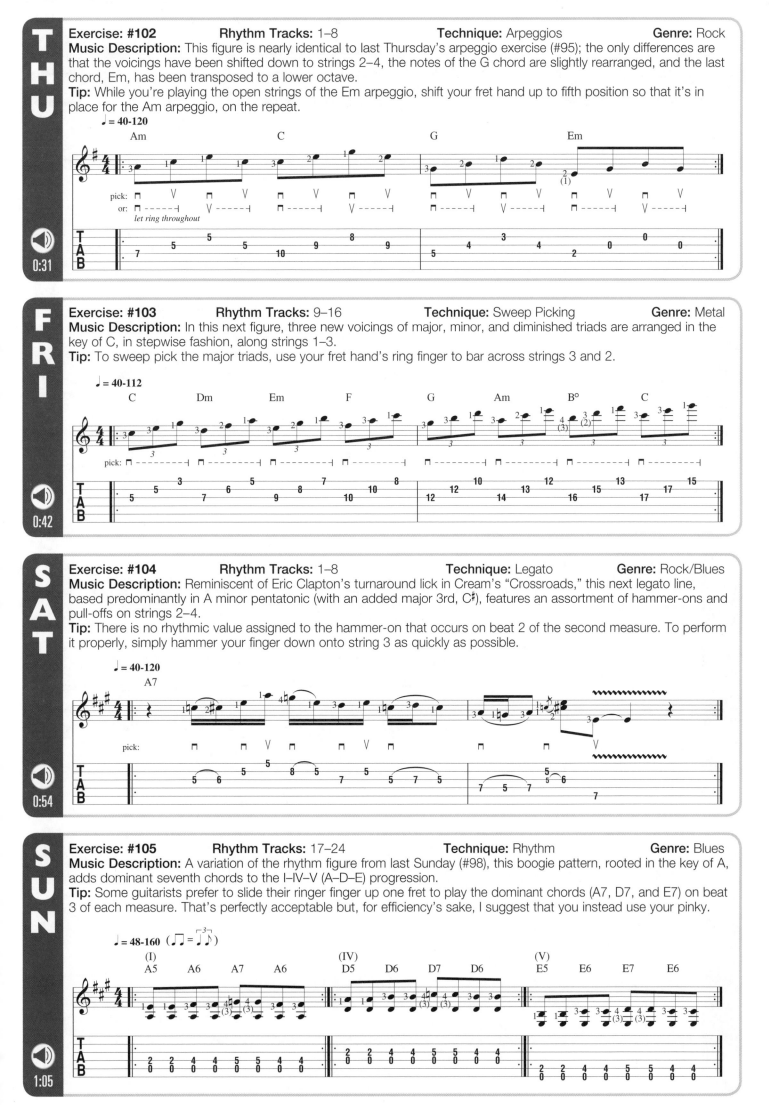

WEEK 16

EXERCISE TRACK 16

MON

Exercise: #106　　　**Rhythm Tracks:** 1–8　　　**Technique:** Alternate Picking　　　**Genre:** Rock

Music Description: This figure reverses the order of the ascending and descending C and Am arpeggios found in Exercise 85.

Tip: Although this exercise starts with a descending C arpeggio, begin with a downstroke, alternating downstokes and upstrokes throughout. Once you're comfortable with this pattern, reverse it and begin with an upstroke.

0:00

TUE

Exercise: #107　　　**Rhythm Tracks:** 17–24　　　**Technique:** String Skipping　　　**Genre:** Blues

Music Description: Constructed from the A blues scale (with an added major 3rd, C♯), this sixths lick, like last Tuesday's exercise (#100), is arranged along strings 1 and 3 exclusively, thus skipping over string 2.

Tip: Only two fret-hand shapes, played with either a middle-index or middle-ring finger combination, are used throughout.

0:11

WED

Exercise: #108　　　**Rhythm Tracks:** 1–8　　　**Technique:** String Bending　　　**Genre:** Rock/Blues

Music Description: A popular bending technique on guitar is the *gradual* bend and/or release. Here, it takes three beats for a whole-step bend on string 2 to reach its apex (bar 1) and 2½ beats to fully release a whole-step bend on string 3 (bar 2).

Tip: Gradual means *gradual*. Execute these bends/releases as smoothly as possible, and be sure to maintain proper intonation.

0:23

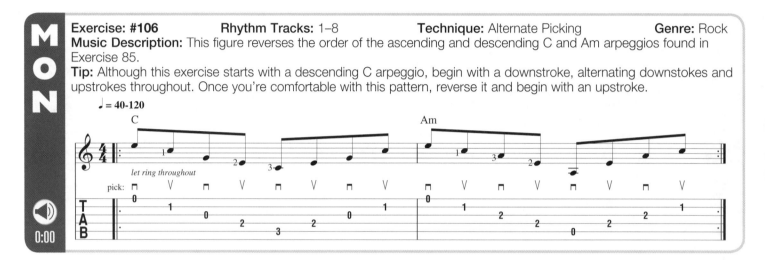

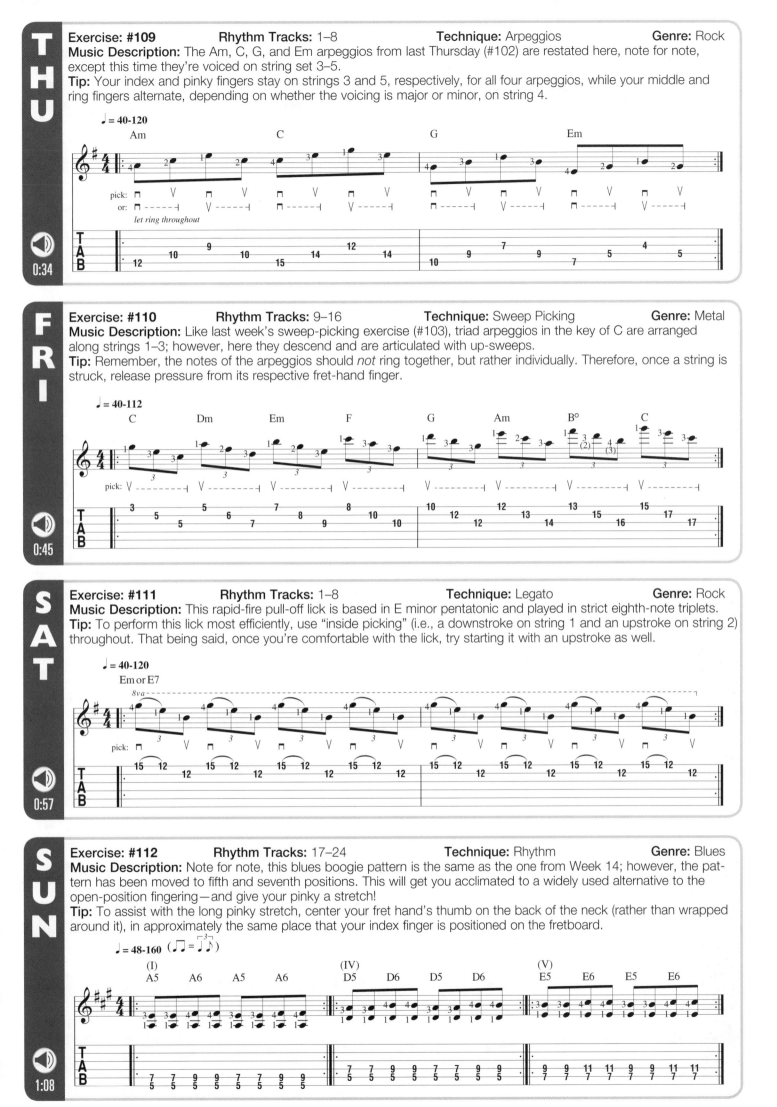

THU

Exercise: #109 **Rhythm Tracks:** 1–8 **Technique:** Arpeggios **Genre:** Rock

Music Description: The Am, C, G, and Em arpeggios from last Thursday (#102) are restated here, note for note, except this time they're voiced on string set 3–5.

Tip: Your index and pinky fingers stay on strings 3 and 5, respectively, for all four arpeggios, while your middle and ring fingers alternate, depending on whether the voicing is major or minor, on string 4.

0:34

FRI

Exercise: #110 **Rhythm Tracks:** 9–16 **Technique:** Sweep Picking **Genre:** Metal

Music Description: Like last week's sweep-picking exercise (#103), triad arpeggios in the key of C are arranged along strings 1–3; however, here they descend and are articulated with up-sweeps.

Tip: Remember, the notes of the arpeggios should *not* ring together, but rather individually. Therefore, once a string is struck, release pressure from its respective fret-hand finger.

0:45

SAT

Exercise: #111 **Rhythm Tracks:** 1–8 **Technique:** Legato **Genre:** Rock

Music Description: This rapid-fire pull-off lick is based in E minor pentatonic and played in strict eighth-note triplets.

Tip: To perform this lick most efficiently, use "inside picking" (i.e., a downstroke on string 1 and an upstroke on string 2) throughout. That being said, once you're comfortable with the lick, try starting it with an upstroke as well.

0:57

SUN

Exercise: #112 **Rhythm Tracks:** 17–24 **Technique:** Rhythm **Genre:** Blues

Music Description: Note for note, this blues boogie pattern is the same as the one from Week 14; however, the pattern has been moved to fifth and seventh positions. This will get you acclimated to a widely used alternative to the open-position fingering—and give your pinky a stretch!

Tip: To assist with the long pinky stretch, center your fret hand's thumb on the back of the neck (rather than wrapped around it), in approximately the same place that your index finger is positioned on the fretboard.

1:08

EXERCISE TRACK 17

Exercise: #113   **Rhythm Tracks:** 1–8   **Technique:** Alternate Picking   **Genre:** Rock
Music Description: Alternate-picked C and Am arpeggios featuring string skipping are once again the order of the day. This time, however, the string-skipping gaps have grown to two and three strings.
Tip: Resist the urge to use a single upstroke to play the notes on the top three strings. Instead, concentrate on alternate picking the entire figure.

0:00

TUE

Exercise: #114   **Rhythm Tracks:** 9–16   **Technique:** String Skipping   **Genre:** Metal
Music Description: The A major scale (A–B–C#–D–E–F#–G#) is arranged in a three-notes-per-string string-skipping exercise, starting in fifth position.
Tip: Notice that there are three distinct fingerings utilized in this exercise, one each for string pairs 1–2, 3–4, and 5–6.

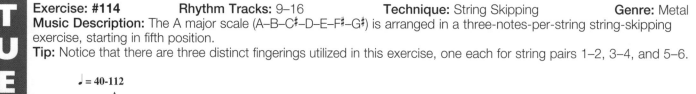

0:11

WED

Exercise: #115   **Rhythm Tracks:** 1–8   **Technique:** String Bending   **Genre:** Rock
Music Description: Quarter-step (bar 1) and multi-step (half and whole; bar 2) double-stop bends pepper this Chuck Berry–inspired lick, featuring notes from both A minor and A major pentatonic.
Tip: The double-stop bends are executed with a ring-finger barre. If you find that too difficult, try using both your ring and pinky fingers to bend the notes.

0:23

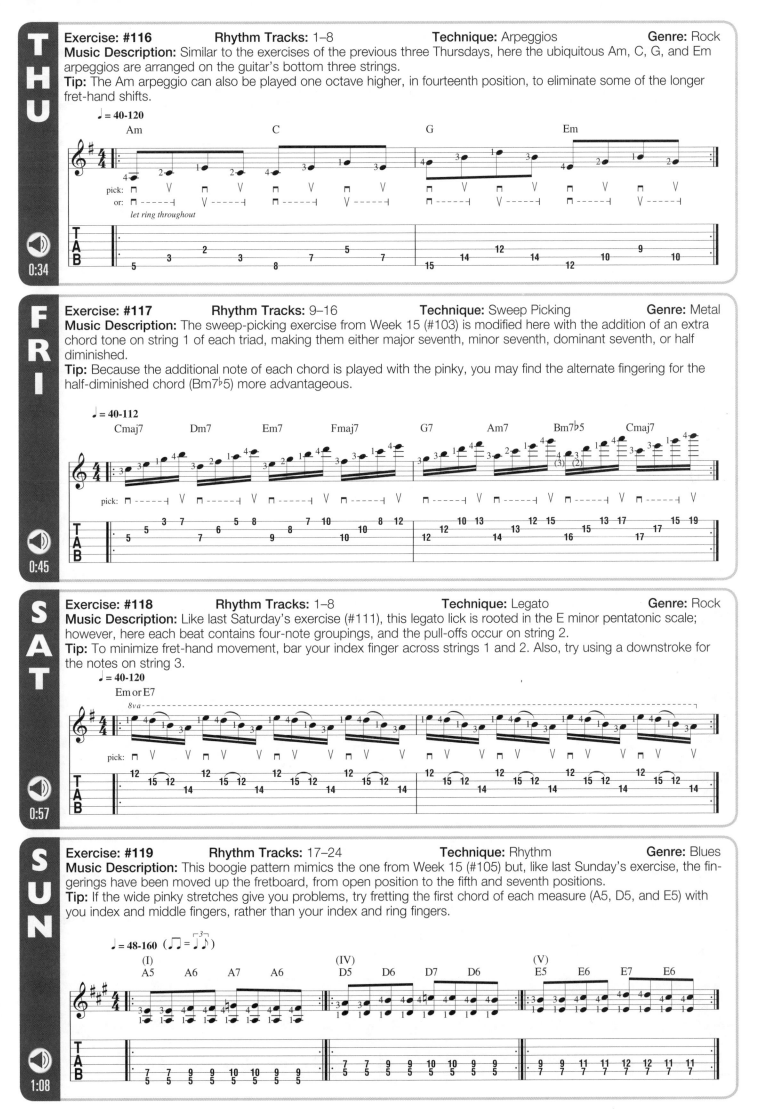

THU

0:34

Exercise: #116   **Rhythm Tracks:** 1–8   **Technique:** Arpeggios   **Genre:** Rock
Music Description: Similar to the exercises of the previous three Thursdays, here the ubiquitous Am, C, G, and Em arpeggios are arranged on the guitar's bottom three strings.
Tip: The Am arpeggio can also be played one octave higher, in fourteenth position, to eliminate some of the longer fret-hand shifts.

FRI

0:45

Exercise: #117   **Rhythm Tracks:** 9–16   **Technique:** Sweep Picking   **Genre:** Metal
Music Description: The sweep-picking exercise from Week 15 (#103) is modified here with the addition of an extra chord tone on string 1 of each triad, making them either major seventh, minor seventh, dominant seventh, or half diminished.
Tip: Because the additional note of each chord is played with the pinky, you may find the alternate fingering for the half-diminished chord (Bm7♭5) more advantageous.

SAT

0:57

Exercise: #118   **Rhythm Tracks:** 1–8   **Technique:** Legato   **Genre:** Rock
Music Description: Like last Saturday's exercise (#111), this legato lick is rooted in the E minor pentatonic scale; however, here each beat contains four-note groupings, and the pull-offs occur on string 2.
Tip: To minimize fret-hand movement, bar your index finger across strings 1 and 2. Also, try using a downstroke for the notes on string 3.

SUN

1:08

Exercise: #119   **Rhythm Tracks:** 17–24   **Technique:** Rhythm   **Genre:** Blues
Music Description: This boogie pattern mimics the one from Week 15 (#105) but, like last Sunday's exercise, the fingerings have been moved up the fretboard, from open position to the fifth and seventh positions.
Tip: If the wide pinky stretches give you problems, try fretting the first chord of each measure (A5, D5, and E5) with you index and middle fingers, rather than your index and ring fingers.

🔊 **EXERCISE TRACK 18**

MON

Exercise: #120   **Rhythm Tracks:** 1–8   **Technique:** Alternate Picking   **Genre:** Rock

Music Description: The only difference between last Monday's exercise (#113) and this one is the order of notes on beats 2 and 4 of each measure. The rearrangement of these notes necessitates another string skip, this time bypassing string 2.

Tip: Notice that in order to change from C to Am, only the ring finger of your fret hand needs to move (third fret of string 5 to second fret of string 3).

🔊 0:00

TUE

Exercise: #121   **Rhythm Tracks:** 9–16   **Technique:** String Skipping   **Genre:** Metal

Music Description: This figure is the descending version of last Tuesday's A major string-skipping exercise (#114).

Tip: If an index-ring-pinky finger combination feels uncomfortable when playing the notes on strings 5 and 6, substitute your middle finger for your ring finger.

🔊 0:11

WED

Exercise: #122   **Rhythm Tracks:** 1–8   **Technique:** String Bending   **Genre:** Rock

Music Description: This riff-based exercise employs quarter-, half-, and whole-step bends on the bass strings, a popular technique in rock and country guitar.

Tip: Whole-step bends on the low strings can be difficult to execute. For the one at the end of this figure, pull the sixth string downward until its pitch matches the open A string.

🔊 0:23

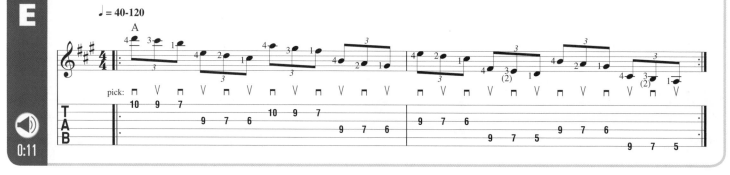

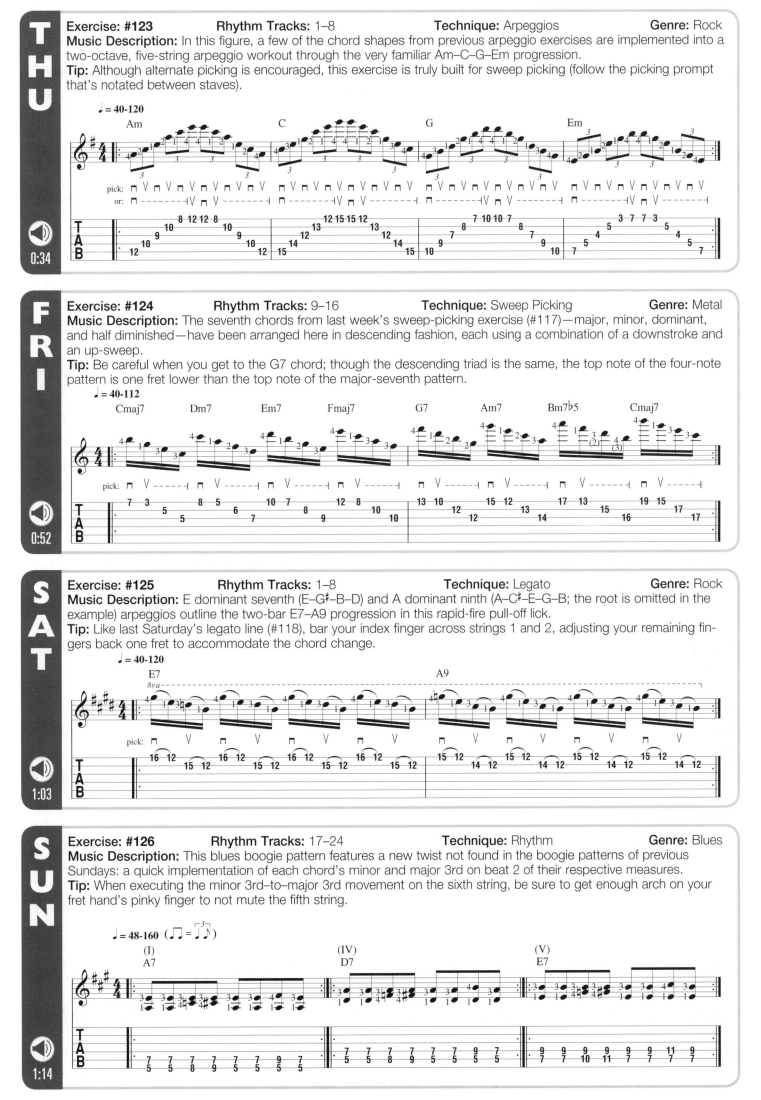

THU

0:34

Exercise: #123 **Rhythm Tracks:** 1–8 **Technique:** Arpeggios **Genre:** Rock

Music Description: In this figure, a few of the chord shapes from previous arpeggio exercises are implemented into a two-octave, five-string arpeggio workout through the very familiar Am–C–G–Em progression.

Tip: Although alternate picking is encouraged, this exercise is truly built for sweep picking (follow the picking prompt that's notated between staves).

FRI

0:52

Exercise: #124 **Rhythm Tracks:** 9–16 **Technique:** Sweep Picking **Genre:** Metal

Music Description: The seventh chords from last week's sweep-picking exercise (#117)—major, minor, dominant, and half diminished—have been arranged here in descending fashion, each using a combination of a downstroke and an up-sweep.

Tip: Be careful when you get to the G7 chord; though the descending triad is the same, the top note of the four-note pattern is one fret lower than the top note of the major-seventh pattern.

SAT

1:03

Exercise: #125 **Rhythm Tracks:** 1–8 **Technique:** Legato **Genre:** Rock

Music Description: E dominant seventh (E–G♯–B–D) and A dominant ninth (A–C♯–E–G–B; the root is omitted in the example) arpeggios outline the two-bar E7–A9 progression in this rapid-fire pull-off lick.

Tip: Like last Saturday's legato line (#118), bar your index finger across strings 1 and 2, adjusting your remaining fingers back one fret to accommodate the chord change.

SUN

1:14

Exercise: #126 **Rhythm Tracks:** 17–24 **Technique:** Rhythm **Genre:** Blues

Music Description: This blues boogie pattern features a new twist not found in the boogie patterns of previous Sundays: a quick implementation of each chord's minor and major 3rd on beat 2 of their respective measures.

Tip: When executing the minor 3rd–to–major 3rd movement on the sixth string, be sure to get enough arch on your fret hand's pinky finger to not mute the fifth string.

EXERCISE TRACK 19

MON

Exercise: #127 **Rhythm Tracks:** 33–40 **Technique:** Alternate Picking **Genre:** Country
Music Description: This country lick is rooted in the C major pentatonic scale (with the addition of one chromatic passing tone, E♭) and features a mixture of fretted and open-string notes.
Tip: Use your index, middle, ring, and pinky fingers to play the notes on the first, second, third, and fourth frets, respectively.

0:00

TUE

Exercise: #128 **Rhythm Tracks:** 9–16 **Technique:** String Skipping **Genre:** Metal
Music Description: This A major string-skipping exercise follows the same concept as Exercise 114, except that, here, the three-note groupings descend on each string before skipping to the new target string.
Tip: Spend extra time working on the position shift that occurs when moving from string 3 to string 2. Although it's only a one-fret shift, it's tricky when playing this type of pattern.

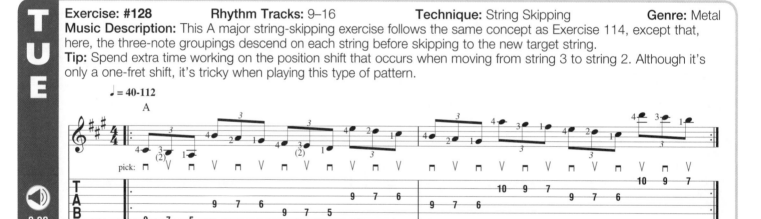

0:09

WED

Exercise: #129 **Rhythm Tracks:** 33–40 **Technique:** String Bending **Genre:** Country
Music Description: Like the exercise from last Wednesday (#122), this figure focuses on bass-string bends. This time, half-step bends are mixed with open strings for a snappy country lick in G.
Tip: Push up, toward the ceiling, when performing these bends, to avoid interference with the adjacent open strings.

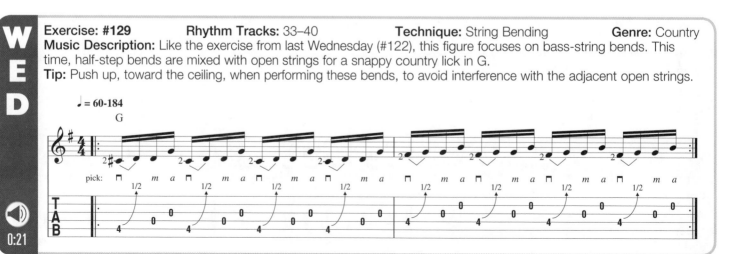

0:21

THU

Exercise: #130 **Rhythm Tracks:** 1–8 **Technique:** Arpeggios **Genre:** Rock
Music Description: A root–3rd–5th–3rd arpeggio pattern is played twice per measure, outlining Am, C, G, and Em chords, respectively, on the guitar's top two strings.
Tip: Not only is this a great arpeggio workout, it happens to be a great alternate-picking exercise, too.

0:30

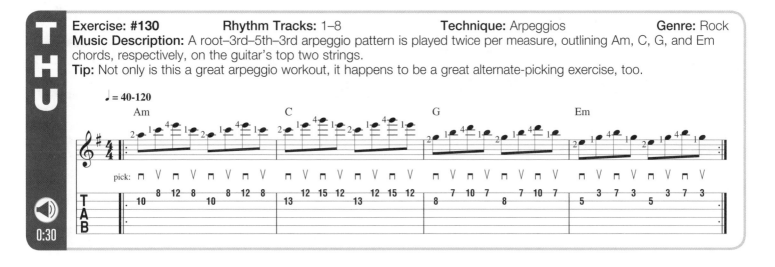

FRI

Exercise: #131 **Rhythm Tracks:** 9–16 **Technique:** Sweep Picking **Genre:** Metal
Music Description: This sweep-picking figure features the same notes as Exercise 117, only here a hammer-on is used in each four-note arpeggio to connect the notes on string 1.
Tip: Take care not to play the first three sweep-picked notes in a triplet rhythm. Instead, these notes should be combined with the hammered note and played in a steady sixteenth-note rhythm.

0:47

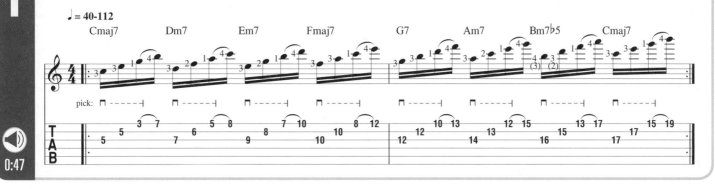

SAT

Exercise: #132 **Rhythm Tracks:** 1–8 **Technique:** Legato **Genre:** Rock
Music Description: A nod to "Eruption," Eddie Van Halen's tapping extravaganza, A major (A–C♯–E), C♯ minor (C♯–E–G♯), B dominant seventh (B–D♯–F♯–A; the root is omitted in the figure), and E major (E–G♯–B) arpeggios are tapped in three-note groupings along string 2.
Tip: The taps can be performed with either your index or middle finger.

0:59

SUN

Exercise: #133 **Rhythm Tracks:** 17–24 **Technique:** Rhythm **Genre:** Blues
Music Description: Guitar legend Buddy Guy popularized this single-note boogie riff while playing the Chicago blues circuit in the 1960s. The line consists of each chord's root (beats 1 and 2), as well as its ♭7th (beat 3) and 5th (beat 4). For example, the line for the A7 chord, in measure 1, contains the notes A (root), A (root octave), G (♭7th), and E (5th).
Tip: All of the notes in this figure should be performed in a staccato manner (i.e., short and crisp).

1:16

EXERCISE TRACK 20

MON

Exercise: #134　　　　**Rhythm Tracks:** 33–40　　　　**Technique:** Alternate Picking　　　　**Genre:** Country
Music Description: Like last Monday's lick (#127), this country line also features the C major pentatonic scale (with an E♭ passing tone); however, this lick predominantly descends the scale, resolving to the root (C) in the second measure.
Tip: Practice each measure separately until you can play through them with no mistakes. Then, link the measures together and play the entire phrase repeatedly.

0:00

(♩ = 60-184)

TUE

Exercise: #135　　　　**Rhythm Tracks:** 9–16　　　　**Technique:** String Skipping　　　　**Genre:** Metal
Music Description: Influenced by last Tuesday's exercise (#128), here the A major scale is arranged into three-note groupings that ascend each string while simultaneously descending the neck vertically via a string-skipping pattern.
Tip: Because of the position shifts that occur between string pairs 1–2 and 3–4, first practice this exercise a half measure at a time to isolate the position shifts.

0:07

(♩ = 40-112)

WED

Exercise: #136　　　　**Rhythm Tracks:** 33–40　　　　**Technique:** String Bending　　　　**Genre:** Country
Music Description: This bass-string bending riff was borrowed from Brad Paisley's bag of tricks. The figure's two chords (B and E) are connected with quick bends of the fifth and sixth strings, at the end of measure 1.
Tip: After playing the B chord, move your index and ring fingers to the sixth and fifth strings, respectively, like you're going to play an F♯ power chord. This will put you in perfect position to attack the bends.

0:19

(♩ = 60-184)

44

THU

🔊 0:28

Exercise: #137   **Rhythm Tracks:** 1–8   **Technique:** Arpeggios   **Genre:** Rock

Music Description: Note for note, this arpeggio exercise is identical to the one from last Thursday (#130); however, here the fingerings have been shifted to string set 2–3.

Tip: The C and G arpeggios use the same finger pattern so simply slide your fret hand down the neck, from seventeenth to twelfth position. The minor arpeggios (Am and Em) also share the same fingering.

FRI

🔊 0:45

Exercise: #138   **Rhythm Tracks:** 9–16   **Technique:** Sweep Picking   **Genre:** Metal

Music Description: The major, minor, dominant, and half-diminished seventh chords from Weeks 17–19 are arranged here into a sweep-picking exercise that features descending arpeggios performed with pull-offs and up-sweeps.

Tip: Think of each four-note arpeggio as being divided in half, with one half featuring a pull-off and the other half featuring a two-note up-sweep.

SAT

🔊 0:57

Exercise: #139   **Rhythm Tracks:** 1–8   **Technique:** Legato   **Genre:** Rock

Music Description: This tapping exercise borrows the A, C♯m, B7, and E arpeggios and triplet rhythms from last Saturday's example (#132) but rearranges the order in which the second and third notes of each arpeggio are played.

Tip: To achieve a consistent attack with each note, push the string down (or up) slightly with your tapping finger before it's released.

SUN

🔊 1:14

Exercise: #140   **Rhythm Tracks:** 17–24   **Technique:** Rhythm   **Genre:** Blues

Music Description: Similar to last Sunday's boogie pattern (#133), this riff incorporates a quick, three-note "tag" to each measure, adding some zest to the aural—and performance—monotony of a 12-bar blues.

Tip: Don't be afraid to mix and match this boogie pattern with the one from last week. It will keep you lines sounding fresh!

45

WEEK 21

EXERCISE TRACK 21

MON

Exercise: #141   **Rhythm Tracks:** 33–40   **Technique:** Alternate Picking   **Genre:** Country
Music Description: The G major pentatonic scale (with a B♭ passing tone) informs this hot country lick, which is similar to the ascending open-position lick from Week 19 (#127).
Tip: Whenever possible, let notes ring together to give the phrase a touch of country "twang".

0:00

TUE

Exercise: #142   **Rhythm Tracks:** 9–16   **Technique:** String Skipping   **Genre:** Metal
Music Description: Similar to the A major patterns of the previous few Tuesdays, the A natural minor scale is arranged into a three-notes-per-string string-skipping exercise. Here, however, the groupings jump a whole octave (A to A, D to D, etc.) when moving from one string to the next.
Tip: These string skips cover more of the neck (two- and three-fret jumps) than the A major scale patterns, so practice each skip separately before playing the entire exercise.

0:07

WED

Exercise: #143   **Rhythm Tracks:** 33–40   **Technique:** String Bending   **Genre:** Country
Music Description: You'll need lots of finger strength—and patience—to pull of this "pedal-steel" lick in C major, a favorite of country pickers.
Tip: Use hybrid picking (a combination of your pick and fingers) to play this lick, plucking the non-bent notes on the second string with your middle finger.

0:19

THU

Exercise: #144   **Rhythm Tracks:** 1–8   **Technique:** Arpeggios   **Genre:** Rock

Music Description: In this exercise, the familiar Am–C–G–Em two-string arpeggio pattern from the previous two Thursdays (#130 and #137) is played in a lower octave, on strings 3 and 4.

Tip: You can use the same three fingers (index, middle, and pinky) for the first three arpeggios simply by adjusting your fingering on string 3 by one fret.

0:28

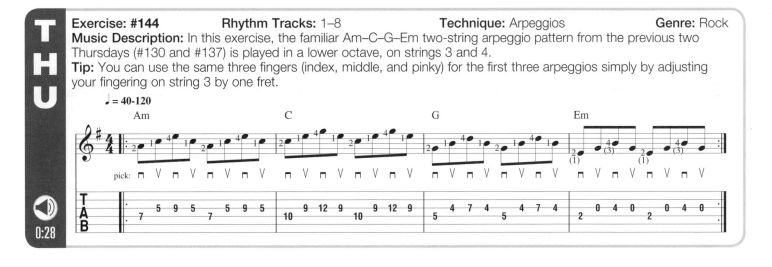

FRI

Exercise: #145   **Rhythm Tracks:** 9–16   **Technique:** Sweep Picking   **Genre:** Metal

Music Description: Major, minor, dominant, and half-diminished seventh chords in the key of C are arranged in a rapid-fire ascending/descending sweep-picking pattern that moves stepwise up the neck on strings 1–3.

Tip: Use back-to-back upstrokes to play the fourth and sixth notes of each six-note arpeggio. (The fifth note is sounded by the pull-off.)

0:45

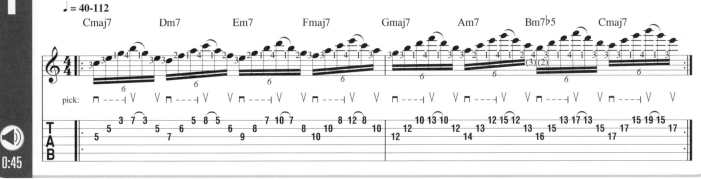

SAT

Exercise: #146   **Rhythm Tracks:** 1–8   **Technique:** Legato   **Genre:** Rock

Music Description: This figure combines the A, C#m, B7, and E arpeggio note sequences from Exercises 132 and 139 into a singular tapping workout.

Tip: Because both hands must move simultaneously, spend extra time working on shifting from the B7 arpeggio to the E major arpeggio.

0:57

SUN

Exercise: #147   **Rhythm Tracks:** 17–24   **Technique:** Rhythm   **Genre:** Blues

Music Description: A nod to Stevie Ray Vaughan's "Pride and Joy," this shuffle pattern features a walk-up of the E major pentatonic scale (E–G#–B–C#–E) that alternates with E major chord stabs.

Tip: Use an exaggerated form of alternated picking, playing the bass notes with a downstroke and the staccato chord stabs with an upstroke.

1:13

EXERCISE TRACK 22

MON

Exercise: #148   **Rhythm Tracks:** 33–40   **Technique:** Alternate Picking   **Genre:** Country
Music Description: Like last week's lick (#141), this phrase is constructed from the G major pentatonic scale (with a B♭ passing tone). Unlike last week's lick, however, this line predominantly descends the scale, resolving to the root (G) on the sixth string.
Tip: Watch out for the adjacent open strings that cross the bar line. These are tricky and will need some extra attention.

0:00

TUE

Exercise: #149   **Rhythm Tracks:** 9–16   **Technique:** String Skipping   **Genre:** Metal
Music Description: The A minor string-skipping exercise from last Tuesday (#142) is arranged here in descending fashion.
Tip: Once your comfortable alternate picking this exercise, try employing pull-offs to articulate the notes.

0:07

WED

Exercise: #150   **Rhythm Tracks:** 33–40   **Technique:** String Bending   **Genre:** Country
Music Description: A whole-step bend is held for an entire measure while notes from the G major scale are struck intermittently between reiterations of the bent note.
Tip: Reinforce your bending (ring) finger with your middle finger, especially when playing the notes on string 1. This will help to keep the bent note in tune. It also requires you to play the 8th-fret C with your index finger.

0:19

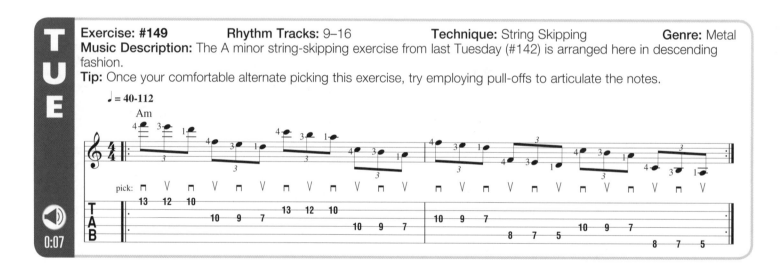

THU

Exercise: #151   **Rhythm Tracks:** 1–8   **Technique:** Arpeggios   **Genre:** Rock

Music Description: In this figure, the arpeggio pattern from last Thursday (#144) is restated, note for note; however, the fret-hand fingerings have been shifted to strings 4 and 5.

Tip: Once you're comfortable alternate picking this exercise, try using legato—a combination of hammer-ons and pull-offs—to articulate the notes on string 4.

0:26

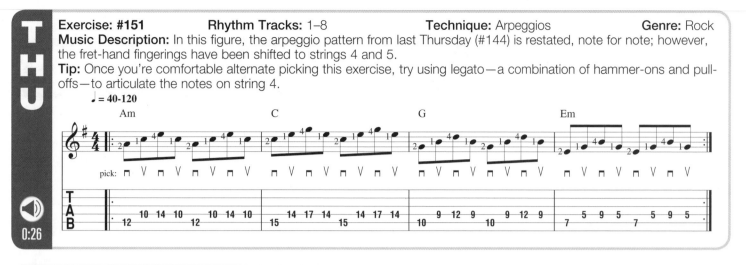

FRI

Exercise: #152   **Rhythm Tracks:** 9–16   **Technique:** Sweep Picking   **Genre:** Metal

Music Description: This neoclassical sweep-picking lick is inspired by Swedish super-picker Yngwie Malmsteen. Here, diminished-seventh arpeggios are "swept" over an E7♭9 chord before resolving to the root of the Am chord.

Tip: All three diminished-seventh arpeggios feature the same finger pattern and move up the neck in minor 3rds (three-fret increments).

0:44

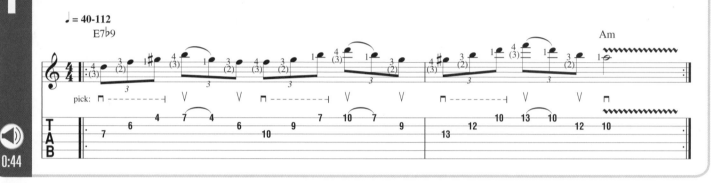

SAT

Exercise: #153   **Rhythm Tracks:** 1–8   **Technique:** Legato   **Genre:** Rock

Music Description: This tapping fest borrows the A, C#m, B7, and E arpeggios from last Saturday's exercise (#146) but flip-flops the note sequences of beats 1 and 2, and 3 and 4, of each measure.

Tip: To prevent unwanted string noise, use the underside of your fret hand's index finger to mute string 1 and the blade of your pick hand to mute strings 3–6.

0:55

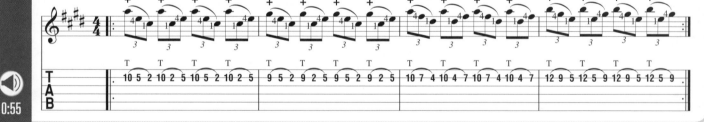

SUN

Exercise: #154   **Rhythm Tracks:** 17–24   **Technique:** Rhythm   **Genre:** Blues

Music Description: In guitar lingo, this blues rhythm is commonly referred to as "sliding 6ths" because of the interval (a 6th) that exists between the top and bottom note of each three-note chord voicing. In fact, this figure is often played with the middle notes of the chords being omitted.

Tip: Voice the D9 and E9 chords like standard dominant-ninth chords, with your fret hand's index finger on fret 4 of the fourth string and fret 6 of the fourth string, respectively. Of course, these notes are voiced only; they should remain silent.

1:13

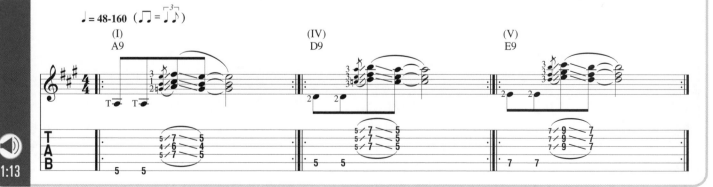

GUITAR
AEROBICS

WEEK 23

EXERCISE TRACK 23

MON

Exercise: #155 **Rhythm Tracks:** 25–32 **Technique:** Alternate Picking **Genre:** Jazz

Music Description: This next exercise features a three-octave, two-notes-per-string G major seventh arpeggio, starting on the seventh degree (F♯) of the chord/scale.

Tip: Notice that the first note, F♯, starts on the "and" of beat 4 (this is called a "pickup" note) and should be picked with an upstroke.

♩ = 56-144 (♫ = ♪♪)

Gmaj7

0:00

TUE

Exercise: #156 **Rhythm Tracks:** 9–16 **Technique:** String Skipping **Genre:** Metal

Music Description: An A minor string-skipping workout similar to the one found in Week 21 (#142) is utilized here, although the three-note groupings now descend on each string while the overall pattern ascends the fretboard.

Tip: The same pinky-ring-index finger combination is used for all six strings.

♩ = 40-112

Am

0:11

WED

Exercise: #157 **Rhythm Tracks:** 33–40 **Technique:** String Bending **Genre:** Country

Music Description: G, F, and C chords (V–IV–I in the key of C) are outlined with a restated pedal-steel lick that moves positionally—from twelfth to tenth to seventh—down the neck.

Tip: Keep your pinky hovering over (or on) strings 1 and 2, and your index and ring fingers hovering over string 3, while you move down the neck. That way, they'll be in place to restate the lick at each stop.

♩ = 60-184

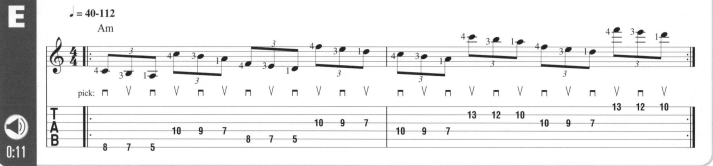

0:23

THU

Exercise: #158   **Rhythm Tracks:** 1–8   **Technique:** Arpeggios   **Genre:** Rock

Music Description: In this figure, the arpeggio pattern used to outline the Am–C–G–Em progressions of the last several Thursdays is restated in a lower octave, on strings 5 and 6.

Tip: The G and Em arpeggios can also be played an octave lower than written, in third and open positions, respectively. Use your ear to guide you.

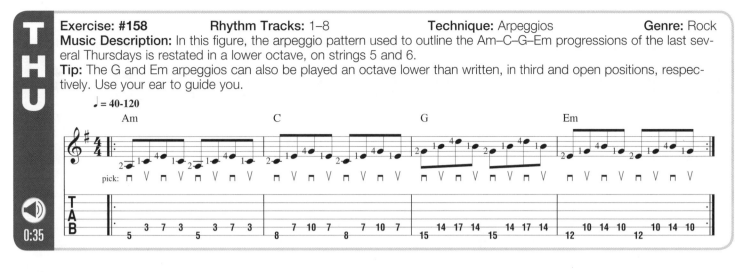

FRI

Exercise: #159   **Rhythm Tracks:** 17–24   **Technique:** Sweep Picking   **Genre:** Blues

Music Description: In this standard A minor pentatonic blues phrase, muted string sweeps lead into whole-step bends in measure 1. This is followed, in measure 2, by a reverse (upwards) sweep at the fifth fret that leads into a quarter-step bend.

Tip: Use the fleshy underside of your pick hand to mute the strings during the sweeps in measure 1.

SAT

Exercise: #160   **Rhythm Tracks:** 1–8   **Technique:** Legato   **Genre:** Rock

Music Description: For this tapping lick, an additional chord tone has been added to the A, C#m, B7 and E arpeggios that were used in the legato exercises of the previous four weeks, changing the rhythms from triplets to sixteenth notes.

Tip: Focus on the sixteenth-note rhythm, taking care not to omit the last note of each four-note grouping and reverting back to the triplet rhythms of previous examples.

SUN

Exercise: #161   **Rhythm Tracks:** 25–32   **Technique:** Rhythm   **Genre:** Jazz

Music Description: A variation of the popular "Charleston" rhythm, this jazz-swing pattern, shown here using voicings of a I–IV–V progression in the key of G major (G7–C9–D9), is prevalent in big-band settings.

Tip: Accent both chord attacks (beat 1 and the "and" of beat 2) in each measure. Also, the first chord of each measure should be played staccato.

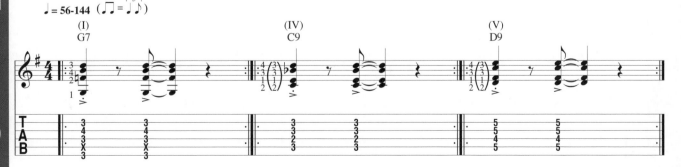

0:35

0:52

1:03

1:14

EXERCISE TRACK 24

MON

Exercise: #162   **Rhythm Tracks:** 25–32   **Technique:** Alternate Picking   **Genre:** Jazz
Music Description: This figure is identical to Exercise 155 from last week except for one note, F♯ (the 7th), which has been lowered a half step, to F (the ♭7th), to make it a G *dominant seventh* arpeggio (G–B–D–F).
Tip: To accommodate the lowered seventh, use your index and ring fingers (rather than your index and middle fingers, as in Exercise 155) to play the notes on strings 2, 4, and 6.

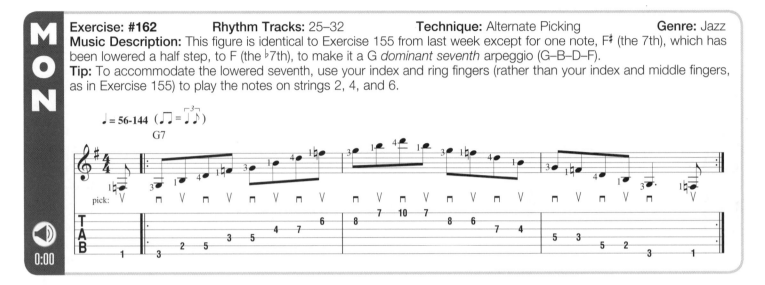

0:00

TUE

Exercise: #163   **Rhythm Tracks:** 9–16   **Technique:** String Skipping   **Genre:** Metal
Music Description: Building on the A minor string-skipping exercises of the previous three weeks, this figure ascends three scale tones on one string before skipping to the next target string.
Tip: After you've become comfortable alternate picking the sequence, try employing hammer-ons to execute the notes on each string.

0:11

WED

Exercise: #164   **Rhythm Tracks:** 1–8   **Technique:** String Bending   **Genre:** Blues
Music Description: This open-position lick combines whole-step (string 3) and half-step (string 1) bends with open strings for a bluesy sound.
Tip: Whole-step bends in open position can be difficult to execute. Wrapping your thumb around the neck will give you a little extra leverage.

0:23

THU

Exercise: #165   **Rhythm Tracks:** 1–8   **Technique:** Arpeggios   **Genre:** Rock

Music Description: A 5th–3rd–root–3rd arpeggio pattern is played twice per measure, outlining the ubiquitous Am–C–G–Em progression.

Tip: Try playing this pattern over other progressions that you know, using the note on string 2, the root, as your positional guide, and then adjusting your fingerings according to whether the chords are major or minor.

♩ = 40-120

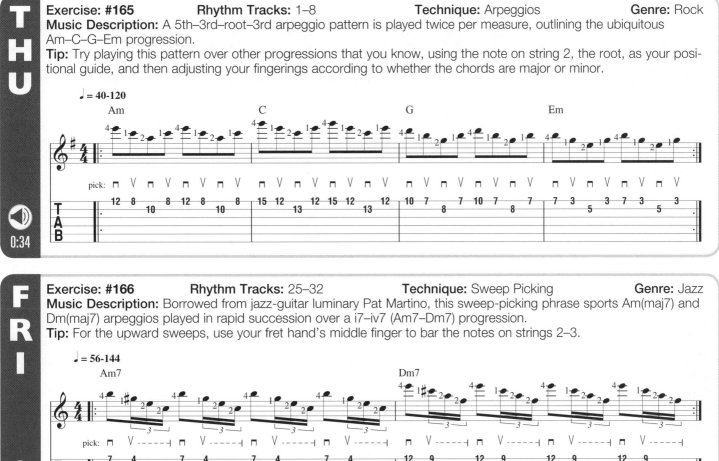

0:34

FRI

Exercise: #166   **Rhythm Tracks:** 25–32   **Technique:** Sweep Picking   **Genre:** Jazz

Music Description: Borrowed from jazz-guitar luminary Pat Martino, this sweep-picking phrase sports Am(maj7) and Dm(maj7) arpeggios played in rapid succession over a i7–iv7 (Am7–Dm7) progression.

Tip: For the upward sweeps, use your fret hand's middle finger to bar the notes on strings 2–3.

♩ = 56-144

0:51

SAT

Exercise: #167   **Rhythm Tracks:** 1–8   **Technique:** Legato   **Genre:** Rock

Music Description: A four-note scalar sequence, featuring notes from the A Dorian (A–B–C–D–E–F♯–G) mode, or, due to the omission of a minor or major 3rd, A Mixolydian (A–B–C♯–D–E–F♯–G) mode, is repeated on each beat of this two-bar tapping phrase.

Tip: After five weeks of tapping exercises, your ring finger is incorporated into the festivities for the first time so concentrate on achieving consistent volume across all four notes.

♩ = 40-120

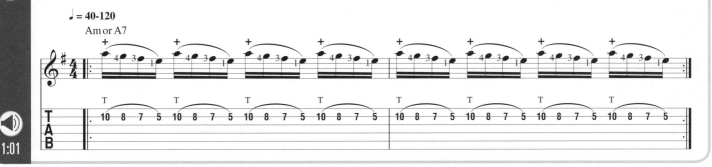

1:01

SUN

Exercise: #168   **Rhythm Tracks:** 25–32   **Technique:** Rhythm   **Genre:** Jazz

Music Description: Illustrated using the I–IV–V (G7–C9–D9) progression from last Sunday (#161), this "four to the bar" comping pattern is another favorite of jazz guitarists in big-band settings.

Tip: All of the chords in this example should be played staccato, with the chords on beats 2 and 4 of each measure receiving accents (i.e., played louder). Also, a popular technique when playing this example, thanks to Count Basie guitarist Freddie Green, is to sound only the lowest three notes of each four-note chord voicing.

♩ = 56-144

1:12

53

WEEK 25

EXERCISE TRACK 25

MON

Exercise: #169   **Rhythm Tracks:** 25–32   **Technique:** Alternate Picking   **Genre:** Jazz
Music Description: The third degree, B, of the G dominant seventh arpeggio pattern from last week (#162) has been lowered a half step to B♭, making it a G minor seventh arpeggio.
Tip: Divide the arpeggio into string pairs (6–5, 4–3, 2–1), using an index-ring/index-pinky finger pattern for each.

0:00

TUE

Exercise: #170   **Rhythm Tracks:** 9–16   **Technique:** String Skipping   **Genre:** Metal
Music Description: In this string-skipping exercise, the C major scale (or A minor, its relative minor scale) is arranged in an ascending, three-notes-per-string pattern on both the first and third strings, completely skipping over string 2.
Tip: Experiment with various ways to finger this exercise. The fingerings notated are merely suggestions.

0:11

WED

Exercise: #171   **Rhythm Tracks:** 1–8   **Technique:** String Bending   **Genre:** Rock/Blues
Music Description: Rooted in the 12th-position E minor pentatonic scale, this lick is a repeating three-note sequence featuring whole-step bends on string 3.
Tip: Use a down-down-up picking pattern to perform each three-note pattern.

0:22

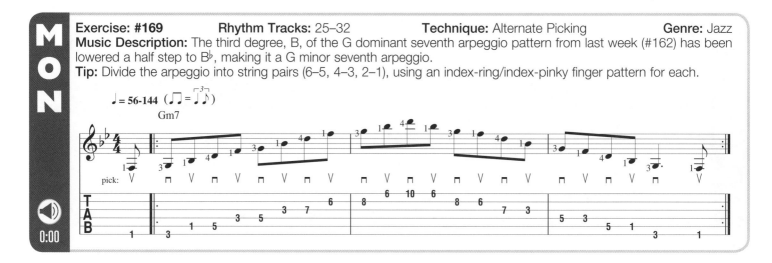

THU

Exercise: #172 **Rhythm Tracks:** 1–8 **Technique:** Arpeggios **Genre:** Rock

Music Description: For this exercise, the Am, C, G, and Em arpeggio patterns from Exercise 165 have been shifted from strings 1 and 2 to strings 2 and 3, resulting in different fingerings.

Tip: As an alternative to alternate picking, use a pull-off to articulate the first two notes of each pattern; pick the two remaining notes.

0:34

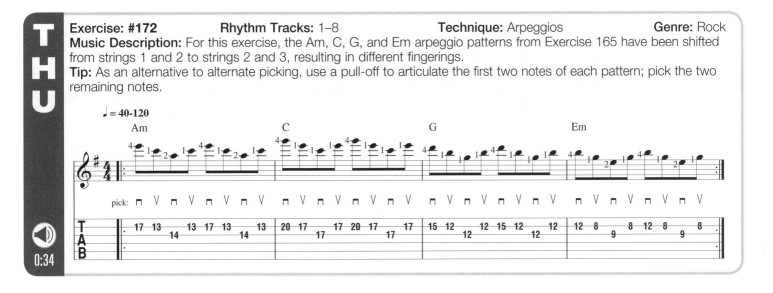

FRI

Exercise: #173 **Rhythm Tracks:** 25–32 **Technique:** Sweep Picking **Genre:** Jazz

Music Description: In this A minor phrase, an upward sweep commonly used by jazz guitarists is employed at the fifth fret.

Tip: Take care not to rush the sweep; it should be played in an even eighth-note-triplet rhythm.

0:51

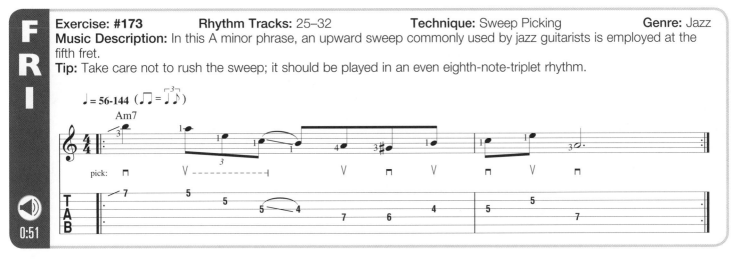

SAT

Exercise: #174 **Rhythm Tracks:** 1–8 **Technique:** Legato **Genre:** Rock

Music Description: The four notes in last week's tapping exercise (E, F#, G, and A) make an encore performance here; however, the note sequence has been reversed, thus hammer-ons are employed after each finger tap.

Tip: If you get bored with hearing the same four notes played over and over, move your tapping finger up and down the neck for aural variety.

1:00

SUN

Exercise: #175 **Rhythm Tracks:** 25–32 **Technique:** Rhythm **Genre:** Jazz

Music Description: Modeled after last week's "four to the bar" example (#168), this swing accompaniment exercise introduces a quick ii7–V7 (Am7–D9) turnaround pattern (bar 4) to the G major progression.

Tip: When playing the G7 chord, flatten your index finger slightly to mute the fifth string. Same goes for your middle finger when playing the Am7 chord.

1:11

WEEK 26

EXERCISE TRACK 26

MON

Exercise: #176   **Rhythm Tracks:** 25–32   **Technique:** Alternate Picking   **Genre:** Jazz

Music Description: In this alternate-picking workout, the arpeggio patterns from the previous three weeks are utilized to navigate a ii–V–I progression in the key of G (Gm7–C7–Fmaj7).

Tip: Don't forget—start with an upstroke on the "and" of beat 4 of the pickup measure. The same note (F) is found at the end of measure 2, leading back to the beginning of the phrase on the repeat.

0:00

TUE

Exercise: #177   **Rhythm Tracks:** 9–16   **Technique:** String Skipping   **Genre:** Metal

Music Description: The C major/A minor string-skipping sequence from last Tuesday's exercise (#170) is used once again, only this time in descending fashion.

Tip: Because of the triplet rhythms, the picking patterns remain consistent (down-up-down or up-down-up) on both strings throughout.

0:13

WED

Exercise: #178   **Rhythm Tracks:** 1–8   **Technique:** String Bending   **Genre:** Rock/Blues

Music Description: This lick is identical to Exercise 164 from Week 24, only here it's performed one octave higher, in 12th position.

Tip: If using your pinky to perform the bends on string 1 proves problematic, switch to your ring finger.

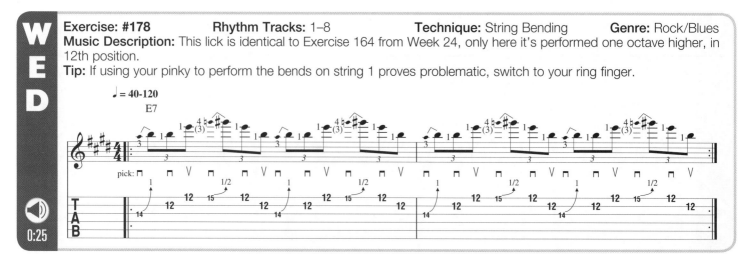

0:25

Exercise: #179   **Rhythm Tracks:** 1–8   **Technique:** Arpeggios   **Genre:** Rock

Music Description: This exercise employs the Am, C, G, and Em arpeggio patterns from the previous two Thursdays (#165 and #172); however, here the patterns are moved down an octave and played on strings 3 and 4.

Tip: Once you're comfortable alternate picking this exercise, starting with a downstroke, reverse direction and start with an upstroke.

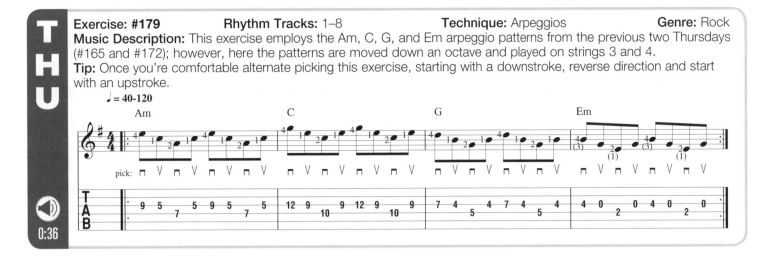

Exercise: #180   **Rhythm Tracks:** 9–16   **Technique:** Sweep Picking   **Genre:** Metal

Music Description: Ascending triad arpeggios in the key of G major, each played with a downwards sweep, are arranged in stepwise fashion along strings 2–4.

Tip: To minimize fret-hand finger movement, keep your index finger barred across strings 2–3 at all times (except for the F#° chord), adding your middle finger to string 3 for the major triads.

Exercise: #181   **Rhythm Tracks:** 1–8   **Technique:** Legato   **Genre:** Rock

Music Description: In this figure, the note sequences in Exercises 167 and 174 have been combined into a single six-note tapping sequence that's played twice per measure.

Tip: A potential problem with long legato lines such as this one is that the notes at the end of the sequence tend to be played at a lower attack volume. To prevent this from occurring, hammer onto the string with the same—or more—authority used for the pull-offs.

Exercise: #182   **Rhythm Tracks:** 25–32   **Technique:** Rhythm   **Genre:** Jazz

Music Description: This example, like the ones from the previous two Sundays, employs the "four to the bar" rhythm technique to play a I–vi–ii–V–iii–VI–ii–V in the key of G (Gmaj–Em7–Am7–D7–Bm7–E7–Am7–D7).

Tip: Three new chord voicings have been introduced in this figure: Gmaj7, Em7, and E7. Get acquainted with the fingerings for each of these chords before attempting to execute all eight chords successively.

WEEK 27

EXERCISE TRACK 27

MON

Exercise: #183   **Rhythm Tracks:** 25–32   **Technique:** Alternate Picking   **Genre:** Jazz
Music Description: The Gm7–C7–Fmaj7 progression from Exercise 176 has been retained for this alternate-picking workout. This time, however, seventh-position, vertical arpeggios are used for the Gm7 and C7 chords before the two-notes-per-string, horizontal pattern is recalled from previous exercises for the Fmaj7 chord.
Tip: Pay strict attention to the fingering suggestions for the most efficient performance of this line.

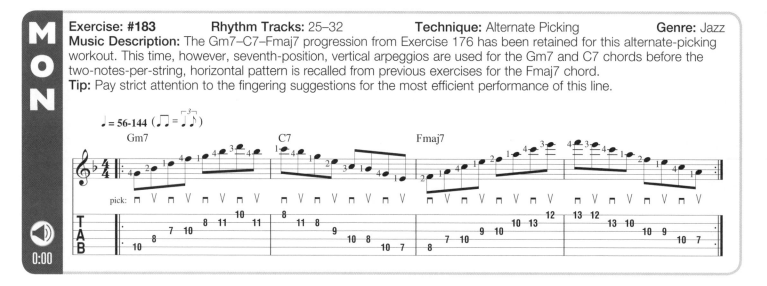

0:00

TUE

Exercise: #184   **Rhythm Tracks:** 9–16   **Technique:** String Skipping   **Genre:** Metal
Music Description: This exercise is similar to the string-skipping sequence presented in Exercise 170, only here each three-note grouping descends along strings 1 and 3 (rather than ascend), skipping over string 2.
Tip: To play this figure most efficiently, use "outside" picking—a down-up-down pattern for string 3 and an up-down-up pattern for string 1.

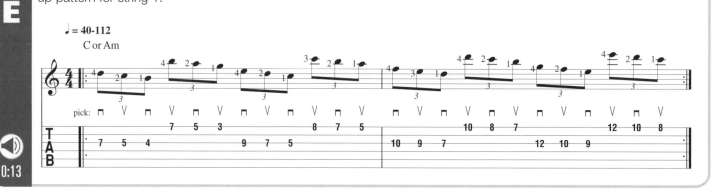

0:13

WED

Exercise: #185   **Rhythm Tracks:** 1–8   **Technique:** String Bending   **Genre:** Rock/Blues
Music Description: Whole-step (strings 2 and 3) and half-step bends (string 1) are the featured techniques in this 12th-position lick.
Tip: Following the whole-step bends on strings 2 and 3, take care not to overextend the half-step bends on string 1.

0:25

THU

Exercise: #186   **Rhythm Tracks:** 1–8   **Technique:** Arpeggios   **Genre:** Rock

Music Description: This figure contains exactly the same notes as last Thursday's exercise (#179), only the fingerings have been shifted to strings 4 and 5.

Tip: If the fingering for the Am arpeggio feels awkward, substitute your ring finger for your middle finger when playing the note on string 5.

0:36

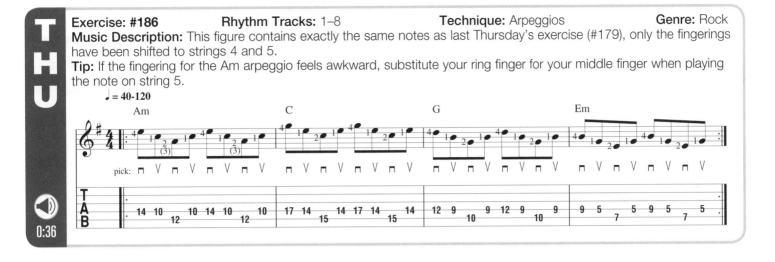

FRI

Exercise: #187   **Rhythm Tracks:** 9–16   **Technique:** Sweep Picking   **Genre:** Metal

Music Description: Here, each diatonic G major arpeggio from last week's sweep-picking exercise (#180) follows a descending sequence on strings 2–4 while simultaneously ascending the neck.

Tip: Once you have the three-string up-sweeps under your fingers, try another picking pattern: play the notes on string 2 with a downstroke and the notes on strings 3–4 with a single upward sweep.

0:54

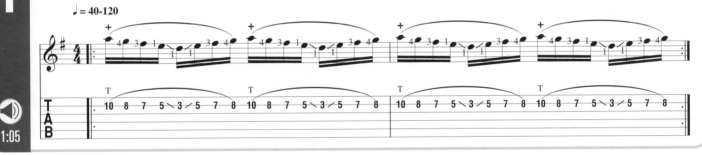

SAT

Exercise: #188   **Rhythm Tracks:** 1–8   **Technique:** Legato   **Genre:** Rock

Music Description: In this workout, an extra note, D, has been added to the tapping exercises from Weeks 24–26. The resulting eight-note sequence spans two beats and includes finger taps, pull-offs, slides, and hammer-ons.

Tip: Don't rush the eight-note groupings! They should be played in a steady sixteenth-note rhythm and counted: "one-ee-and-uh, two-ee-and-uh," etc.

1:05

SUN

Exercise: #189   **Rhythm Tracks:** 25–32   **Technique:** Rhythm   **Genre:** Jazz

Music Description: This jazzy number in G major, featuring the "four to the bar" rhythm pattern from the past several Sundays, walks up the neck in stepwise fashion (from Gmaj7 to Am7) before a nifty turnaround sequence in measure 2 (Am7–D7♯9/D7♭9) sends the sequence back to the beginning.

Tip: When voicing the D7♯9 chord, bar your fret hand's index finger across strings 2–4. That way, it'll be in place for the D7♭9 chord when you lift your pinky finger.

1:17

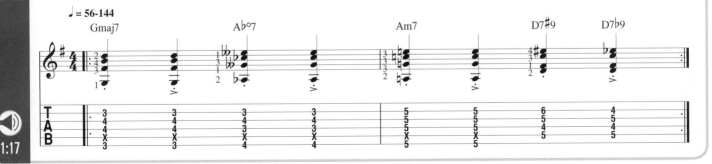

WEEK 28

MON

Exercise: #190   **Rhythm Tracks:** 25–32   **Technique:** Alternate Picking   **Genre:** Jazz

Music Description: In this next alternate-picking exercise, arpeggios and scale fragments are used to navigate the familiar ii–V–I progression in the key of F (Gm7–C7–Fmaj7).

Tip: As always, once you're comfortable playing the line by starting with a downstroke, reverse the sequence and start with an upstroke.

0:00

TUE

Exercise: #191   **Rhythm Tracks:** 9–16   **Technique:** String Skipping   **Genre:** Metal

Music Description: Similar to the string-skipping exercises of the previous three weeks, this figure diatonically descends the C major/A minor scale, while each three-note grouping ascends strings 1 and 3.

Tip: Focus on the index finger of your fret hand, using it to guide your hand to the first note of each new three-note grouping.

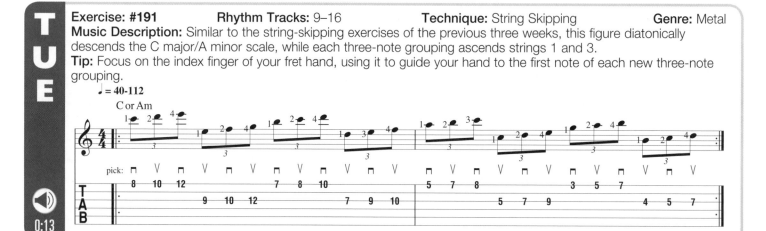

0:13

WED

Exercise: #192   **Rhythm Tracks:** 1–8   **Technique:** String Bending   **Genre:** Rock/Blues

Music Description: The E minor pentatonic scale supplies the notes for this rapid-fire bending lick, which features whole-step bends on strings 2 and 3.

Tip: To perform this lick most efficiently, utilize your pinky for the hammer/pull on string 1 and the bend on string 2, and your ring finger for the bend on string 3.

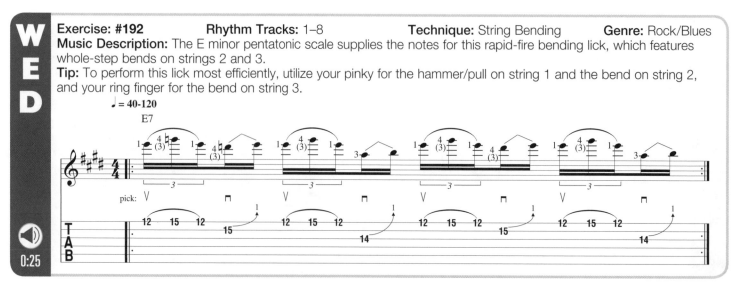

0:25

THU

🔊 0:33

Exercise: #193   **Rhythm Tracks:** 1–8   **Technique:** Arpeggios   **Genre:** Rock
Music Description: These arpeggio patterns—although played on strings 5 and 6 (rather than 4 and 5) with two patterns (Am and C) fretted an octave lower—are, note for note, identical to the ones from last Thursday (#186).
Tip: Your ring finger may be a better option than your middle finger for the Em arpeggio's sixth-string note.

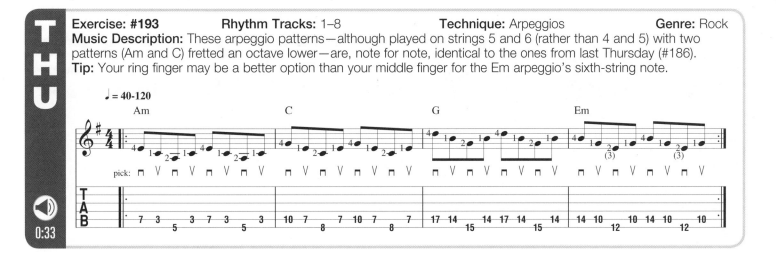

FRI

🔊 0:49

Exercise: #194   **Rhythm Tracks:** 9–16   **Technique:** Sweep Picking   **Genre:** Metal
Music Description: In this figure, extensions have been added to the diatonic G major triads from the sweep-picking exercises in Weeks 26 and 27, making them either major, minor, dominant, or half-diminished seventh-chord arpeggios.
Tip: Spend extra time on the Gmaj7 arpeggio and get comfortable with the wide finger stretch on string 2 before moving on to the rest of the exercise, where you'll encounter less-severe stretches.

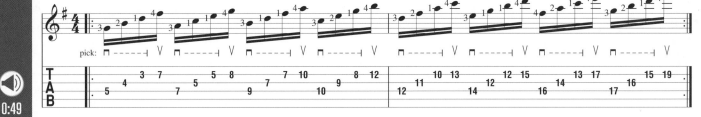

SAT

🔊 1:01

Exercise: #195   **Rhythm Tracks:** 1–8   **Technique:** Legato   **Genre:** Rock
Music Description: A–E–F♯ and A–E–G note groupings, played with a tap/pull/hammer sequence in steady triplets, alternate on each beat, giving your fret-hand ring and pinky fingers a workout.
Tip: Once you have this figure under your fingers, try using your middle and ring fingers to play the notes on frets 7 and 8, respectively, to help improve fret-hand dexterity.

SUN

🔊 1:11

Exercise: #196   **Rhythm Tracks:** 33–40   **Technique:** Rhythm   **Genre:** Country
Music Description: This country accompaniment pattern, played over a C–G7–C progression, features a quarter-note root–5th bass line that alternates with chord partials strummed in eighth notes.
Tip: For the C-chord bass line, move your fret hand's ring finger back and forth between string 5 and string 6. No finger movement is necessary for the G7-chord bass line.

61

WEEK 29

EXERCISE TRACK 29

MON

Exercise: #197   **Rhythm Tracks:** 9–16   **Technique:** Alternate Picking   **Genre:** Metal
Music Description: Major and minor triad arpeggios arranged in triplet rhythms in second position provide the alternate-picking challenge in this neo-classical rock/metal melody.
Tip: Because this is an alternate-picking exercise, fight the temptation to randomly insert upstrokes or downstrokes when it's convenient. Instead, stay true to the picking directions provided between the notation and tab staves.

0:00

TUE

Exercise: #198   **Rhythm Tracks:** 9–16   **Technique:** String Skipping   **Genre:** Metal
Music Description: Here, the three-notes-per-string C major/A minor string-skipping concept of the past several weeks has been moved from strings 1 and 3 to strings 2 and 4, thus posing new fingering challenges.
Tip: Use the suggested fingerings as a guide, but feel free to experiment with your own finger combinations, using whichever feels most natural.

0:17

WED

Exercise: #199   **Rhythm Tracks:** 1–8   **Technique:** String Bending   **Genre:** Blues
Music Description: B.B. King provides the inspiration for this lick in A, which features, quarter-, half-, and whole-step bends performed exclusively on string 1.
Tip: The entire phrase can be performed with just your index and ring fingers, playing notes at the eighth and tenth frets, respectively.

0:28

THU

Exercise: #200   **Rhythm Tracks:** 1–8   **Technique:** Arpeggios   **Genre:** Rock

Music Description: In this figure, familiar patterns found in previous exercises are employed in a three-octave, horizontal Am arpeggio.

Tip: Although you'll be tempted to play this exercise in triplets (patterns of three), it should be performed in an even eighth-note rhythm.

0:41

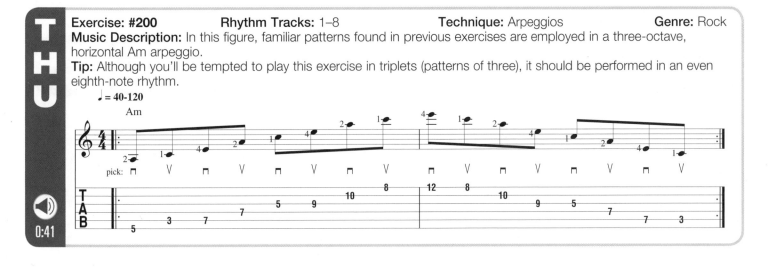

FRI

Exercise: #201   **Rhythm Tracks:** 9–16   **Technique:** Sweep Picking   **Genre:** Metal

Music Description: Each seventh-chord arpeggio from Exercise 194 is arranged here in descending order while the sequence simultaneously ascends the neck.

Tip: After playing the Gmaj7 arpeggio, let your pinky finger be your guide as you move up the neck to each new destination (fret 8, fret 10, fret 12, etc.).

0:52

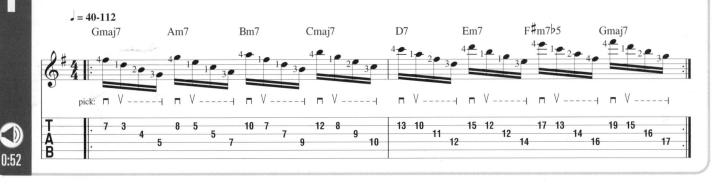

SAT

Exercise: #202   **Rhythm Tracks:** 1–8   **Technique:** Legato   **Genre:** Rock

Music Description: Ascending legato slides, rooted in the E natural minor scale (E–F#–G–A–B–C–D) and performed exclusively on string 2, are the focus of this exercise.

Tip: Put enough arch on your fret hand's middle finger so as not to mute the high E–string drone.

1:03

SUN

Exercise: #203   **Rhythm Tracks:** 33–40   **Technique:** Rhythm   **Genre:** Country

Music Description: This country accompaniment pattern is quite similar to last Sunday's exercise (#196). The only difference is the bass-line hammer-ons that occur on beat 3 of each measure.

Tip: Experiment with mixing and matching this figure with the one from last Sunday. For example, alternate between last week's root–5th bass line and this week's hammer-on bass line every measure.

1:13

63

EXERCISE TRACK 30

MON

Exercise: #204 **Rhythm Tracks:** 9–16 **Technique:** Alternate Picking **Genre:** Metal

Music Description: This figure is identical to last Monday's exercise (#197), only the fingerings for the arpeggios in measures 2–4 have been displaced to upper regions of the neck, presenting new alternate-picking challenges.

Tip: Practice this figure very gradually, working on three notes (one beat) at a time. Then, string it all together and practice the entire exercise at the various tempos provided.

0:00

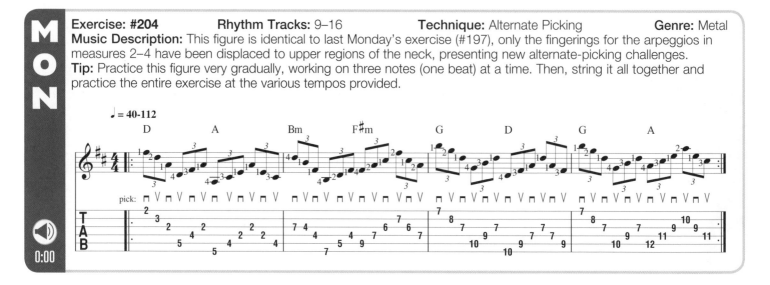

TUE

Exercise: #205 **Rhythm Tracks:** 9–16 **Technique:** String Skipping **Genre:** Metal

Music Description: Last Tuesday's ascending C major/A minor string-skipping exercise (#198) is arranged here in descending fashion.

Tip: Spend extra time working on the last two beats of measure 2, where an odd fingering combined with the string skip make for a tricky maneuver.

0:17

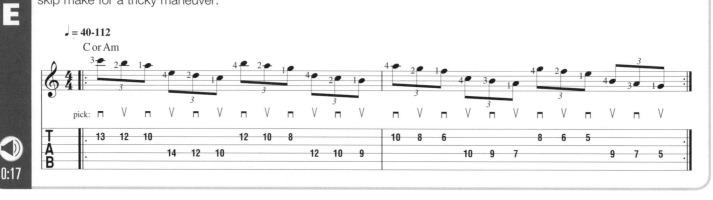

WED

Exercise: #206 **Rhythm Tracks:** 1–8 **Technique:** String Bending **Genre:** Blues

Music Description: Like last Wednesday's lick (#199), this one, too, is inspired by B.B. King and features multiple bends of various steps (quarter, half, and whole) played on string 1.

Tip: Because of the three different types of bends, getting proper intonation for each bend is challenging; therefore, spend extra time working on bending each note to its proper pitch before attempting to play the entire phrase.

0:28

THU

0:44

Exercise: #207 **Rhythm Tracks:** 1–8 **Technique:** Arpeggios **Genre:** Rock
Music Description: Similar to last Thursday's exercise (#200), this example juxtaposes a basic three-note C major chord across the neck horizontally. The end result is a three-octave C major arpeggio.
Tip: The finger pattern for each three-note arpeggio sequence is repeated every other string.

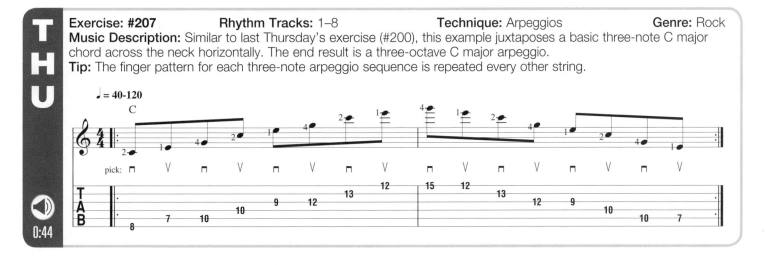

FRI

0:54

Exercise: #208 **Rhythm Tracks:** 9–16 **Technique:** Sweep Picking **Genre:** Metal
Music Description: Borrowing its notes and patterns from Exercise 194, this sweep-picking example, featuring diatonic seventh-chord arpeggios in the key of G major, adds one new twist: a hammer-on.
Tip: If you find you're having trouble with the hammer-ons, practice each one independently—without the sweeps—over and over. Once you feel comfortable with the hammer-ons, add the sweeps and play the entire sequence.

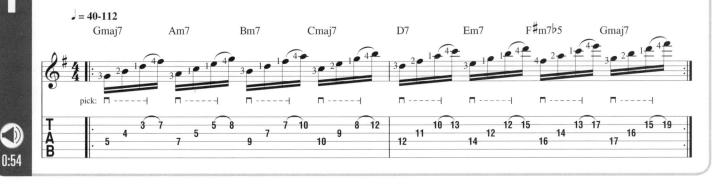

SAT

1:05

Exercise: #209 **Rhythm Tracks:** 1–8 **Technique:** Legato **Genre:** Rock
Music Description: Also featuring legato slides, this figure is the descending version of last Saturday's E minor drone riff.
Tip: Use the fingernail of your fret hand's middle finger to mute string 3 while simultaneously fretting the notes on string 2 with that finger's tip.

SUN

1:16

Exercise: #210 **Rhythm Tracks:** 33–40 **Technique:** Rhythm **Genre:** Country
Music Description: This country rhythm pattern combines elements from Exercises 196 and 203—such as chord partials, the C–G7–C progression, and the root–5th and hammer-on bass lines—with single-note "walk-ups" and a "walk-down."
Tip: For the walk-ups and walk-down, use your fret hand's ring finger for the notes on fret 3 of the fifth and sixth strings, and your middle finger for the note on fret 2 of the fifth string.

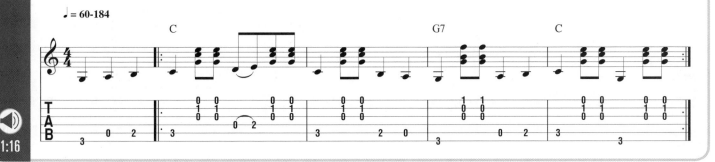

WEEK 31

EXERCISE TRACK 31

MON

Exercise: #211   **Rhythm Tracks:** 9–16   **Technique:** Alternate Picking   **Genre:** Metal
Music Description: The chord changes used in the alternate-picking exercises from the previous two weeks have been arranged here into a sixteenth-note, string-skipping workout.
Tip: Although much of your attention will be dedicated to this figure's string-skipping challenges, don't forget to also concentrate on the *technique du jour*: alternate picking.

0:00

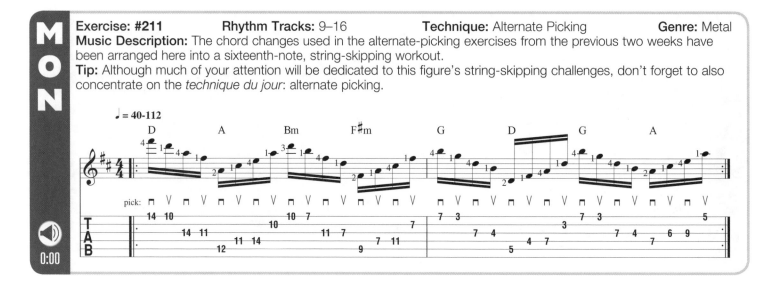

TUE

Exercise: #212   **Rhythm Tracks:** 9–16   **Technique:** String Skipping   **Genre:** Metal
Music Description: Similar to the string-skipping exercise from Week 29 (#198), the C major/A minor scale is arranged here in descending three-note groupings that simultaneously ascend strings 2 and 4.
Tip: The first two beats of the exercise will pose the biggest challenge, so focus on those first.

0:11

WED

Exercise: #213   **Rhythm Tracks:** 1–8   **Technique:** String Bending   **Genre:** Blues
Music Description: This Stevie Ray Vaughan–inspired lick builds on the bending workouts of the previous two weeks (#199 and #206), introducing a quarter-step double-stop bend in measure 1.
Tip: To play the first-string bends that succeed notes from the same fret of the adjacent, second string, use your ring finger for the former and your middle finger for the latter.

0:22

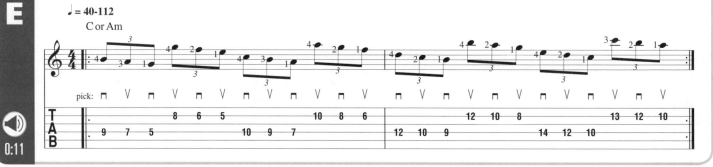

THU

Exercise: #214   **Rhythm Tracks:** 1–8   **Technique:** Arpeggios   **Genre:** Rock

Music Description: This three-octave G major arpeggio climbs the neck horizontally—starting in second position, moving to fourth position, and ending in seventh position—before reversing direction and descending the pattern.

Tip: There are three distinct position shifts in this example, as indicated in the fingerings that are notated.

0:38

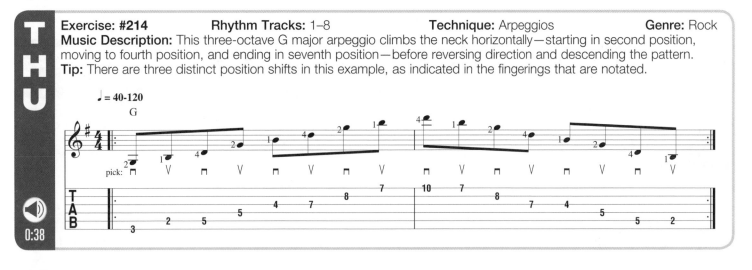

FRI

Exercise: #215   **Rhythm Tracks:** 9–16   **Technique:** Sweep Picking   **Genre:** Metal

Music Description: This example is similar to last week's sweep-picking exercise (#208), only the notes of each arpeggio now descend, and the hammer-on has (naturally) been replaced with a pull-off to articulate the notes on string 2.

Tip: You'll be inclined to sweep the last three notes of each four-note grouping, but don't do it! Instead, play the arpeggios as written, with a pull-off connecting the first two notes and an upward sweep articulating the last two.

0:49

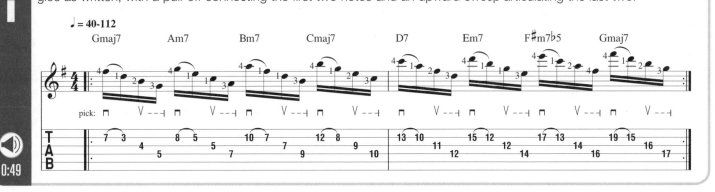

SAT

Exercise: #216   **Rhythm Tracks:** 1–8   **Technique:** Legato   **Genre:** Rock

Music Description: Similar to Exercises 202 and 209, this E minor drone riff, played in steady sixteenth-notes, gradually climbs the neck via a combination of ascending and descending legato slides.

Tip: To further reinforce the riff's tonality in your mind, pluck the open low E string, letting it ring while you play the riff on the top two strings.

1:00

SUN

Exercise: #217   **Rhythm Tracks:** 41–48   **Technique:** Rhythm   **Genre:** Funk

Music Description: Like many funk rhythms, this figure is based on a steady stream of sixteenth notes. Here, a four-note voicing of an E9 chord, played on the top four strings, alternates every beat with string mutes, which are an essential element of funk guitar.

Tip: To properly execute the mutes, simply release the pressure that your fret hand has applied to the E9, leaving your index and ring fingers on the strings with just enough pressure so that a percussive sound is created.

1:11

WEEK 32

EXERCISE TRACK 32

MON

Exercise: #218 **Rhythm Tracks:** 9–16 **Technique:** Alternate Picking **Genre:** Metal
Music Description: The arpeggios from the alternate-picking exercises of the previous three weeks are arranged here along strings 1 and 2 exclusively.
Tip: Although the fret-hand fingerings change to accommodate for major or minor chords, the picking pattern is consistent throughout.

0:00

TUE

Exercise: #219 **Rhythm Tracks:** 9–16 **Technique:** String Skipping **Genre:** Metal
Music Description: Building on the string-skipping exercises of the past several weeks, this figure climbs three steps of the C major/A minor scale on the second string before skipping to the fourth string and repeating the sequence. The pattern is then repeated as it moves horizontally down the neck.
Tip: Although the figure suggests starting with a downstroke, you may find it advantageous to start with an upstroke.

0:10

WED

Exercise: #220 **Rhythm Tracks:** 1–8 **Technique:** String Bending **Genre:** Blues
Music Description: Like last Wednesday's lick (#213), this bending workout is inspired by Stevie Ray Vaughan, although there's a higher concentration of string manipulations in this example.
Tip: A position shift occurs in measure 4. To accommodate this move, use your index finger for the bend on beat 1, and then quickly shift it to the fifth fret to play the subsequent note.

0:22

THU · 0:38

Exercise: #221   **Rhythm Tracks:** 1–8   **Technique:** Arpeggios   **Genre:** Rock

Music Description: Starting at the twelfth fret of string 6, this Em arpeggio pattern covers three octaves and all six strings before reversing course and climbing back down the neck.

Tip: Experiment with the suggested fingerings (one with your middle finger; the other with your ring finger), and use the one that feels most natural.

FRI · 0:49

Exercise: #222   **Rhythm Tracks:** 9–16   **Technique:** Sweep Picking   **Genre:** Metal

Music Description: Elements from the sweep-picking exercises of Weeks 26–31 are employed here to produce a "notey" workout featuring sextuplet rhythms (six notes per beat) and seventh-chord arpeggios diatonic to G major.

Tip: As an alternative to the picking directions notated between staves, try employing a hammer-on/pull-off combination to connect the three notes on string 2, which will eliminate the first upstroke of each arpeggio.

SAT · 1:00

Exercise: #223   **Rhythm Tracks:** 1–8   **Technique:** Legato   **Genre:** Rock

Music Description: Taking its melodic cue from the legato exercises of Weeks 29–31 (i.e., the E natural minor scale), this exercise employs octave shapes, sixteenth notes, and legato slides to ascend the neck, letting the low E string ring along the way.

Tip: To correctly execute the octave shapes, use the fleshy underside of your fret hand's index finger to mute the fourth string.

SUN · 1:11

Exercise: #224   **Rhythm Tracks:** 41–48   **Technique:** Rhythm   **Genre:** Funk

Music Description: This funk rhythm pattern takes the main elements from Exercise 217 (e.g., sixteenth-note rhythms, E9 chord, string mutes) and adds a half-step chordal slide to beats 1 and 3 of each measure.

Tip: Use the underside of your fret hand's middle finger, which is not part of the chord voicing, to mute strings 5 and 6 —not for a percussive sound, but rather to prevent unwanted string noise.

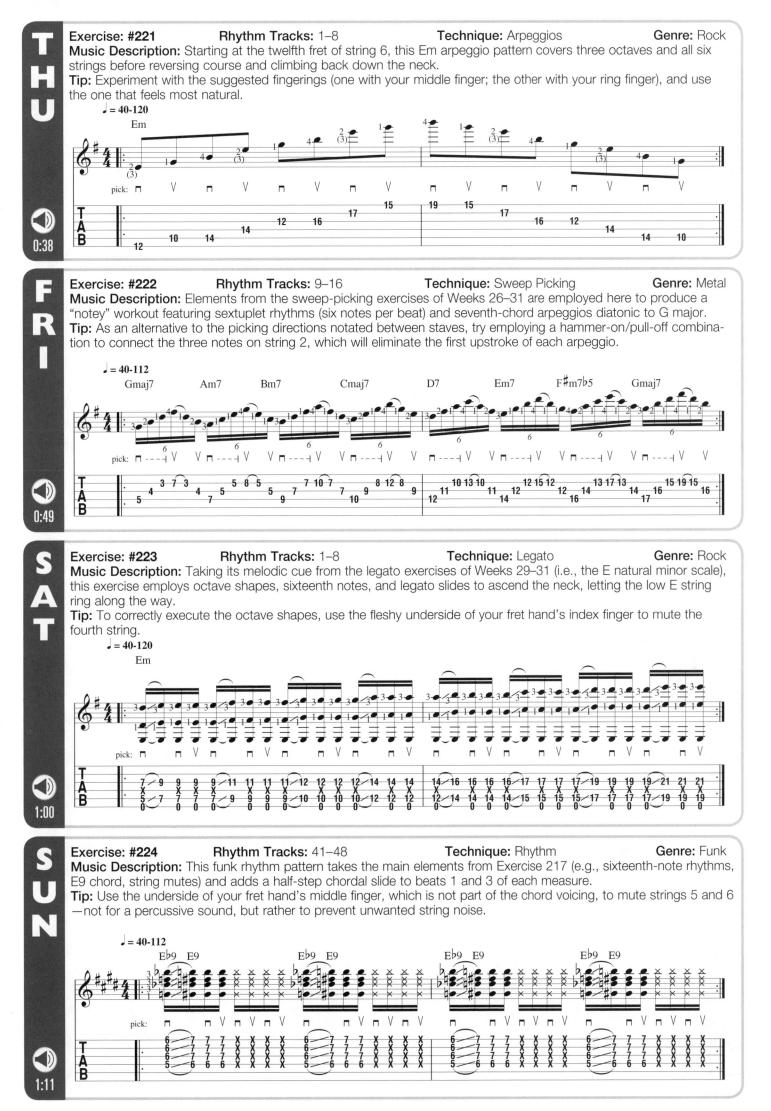

WEEK 33

EXERCISE TRACK 33

MON

Exercise: #225 **Rhythm Tracks:** 9–16 **Technique:** Alternate Picking **Genre:** Metal
Music Description: The same concepts addressed in last week's exercise (#118) are present here; only the note order has been modified to present new alternate-picking challenges.
Tip: Because the middle finger frets all of the notes on the second string, keep it on (or hovering over) that string throughout the exercise.

0:00

TUE

Exercise: #226 **Rhythm Tracks:** 9–16 **Technique:** String Skipping **Genre:** Metal
Music Description: For this exercise, the C major/A minor string-skipping concept you've been working on the last several weeks is utilized once again; however, the patterns have been moved to strings 3 and 5.
Tip: If you're playing an electric guitar (for your hands' sake, I hope you are!), add a little distortion to your tone, which will make the notes easier to articulate.

0:11

WED

Exercise: #227 **Rhythm Tracks:** 33–40 **Technique:** String Bending **Genre:** Country
Music Description: This country lick, played over a C7 chord, features notes from the C major and C minor pentatonic scales and sports a pedal-steel phrase in measures 2 and 3.
Tip: The last note of measure 2 should ring with the bent note in measure 3; therefore, use your middle finger to fret the stationary note and your index finger to perform the bend.

0:21

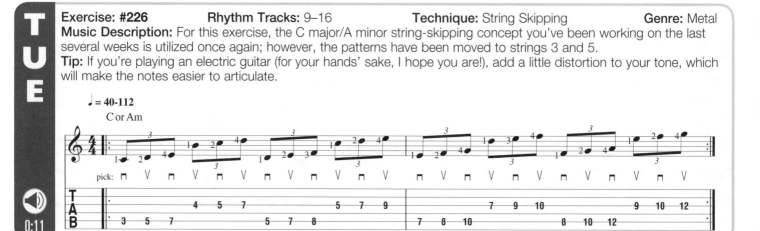

THU — 0:30

Exercise: #228   **Rhythm Tracks:** 25–32   **Technique:** Arpeggios   **Genre:** Jazz

Music Description: An Amaj7 arpeggio, arranged in a three-octave, two-notes-per-string pattern, is the foundation for this figure.

Tip: Don't let the two-notes-per-string pattern dictate the rhythm; this exercise should be played in strict triplets throughout.

FRI — 0:39

Exercise: #229   **Rhythm Tracks:** 9–16   **Technique:** Sweep Picking   **Genre:** Metal

Music Description: Ascending triad arpeggios, diatonic to the key of D major, climb the neck along strings 3–5 and are individually articulated with a single downward sweep.

Tip: The wound D, A, and low-E strings (and perhaps the G string, if you're brave enough!) present a greater challenge than unwound strings with respect to sweep picking. Consequently, you may need to spend considerably more time practicing this exercise and the exercises to follow.

SAT — 0:50

Exercise: #230   **Rhythm Tracks:** 1–8   **Technique:** Legato   **Genre:** Rock

Music Description: This exercise is the descending version of last Saturday's legato figure (#223). The E natural minor scale is once again the melodic source, while octave shapes and legato slides provide the techniques.

Tip: Because this figure shares the same notes as the D Mixolydian mode (D–E–F♯–G–A–B–C), you can try playing the open D string along with the octave shapes, muting the low E string, for a D dominant-seventh tonality.

SUN — 1:01

Exercise: #231   **Rhythm Tracks:** 41–48   **Technique:** Rhythm   **Genre:** Funk

Music Description: This funk figure, which retains the half-step chordal slide (E♭9 to E9) and sixteenth-note pulse from Exercise 224, adds a syncopated rhythm to the chord stabs and string mutes, and introduces an E13 chord, played staccato, on beat 4 of the second measure.

Tip: To voice the E13 chord, simply maintain the preceding E9 voicing and add your pinky to fret 9 of the first string.

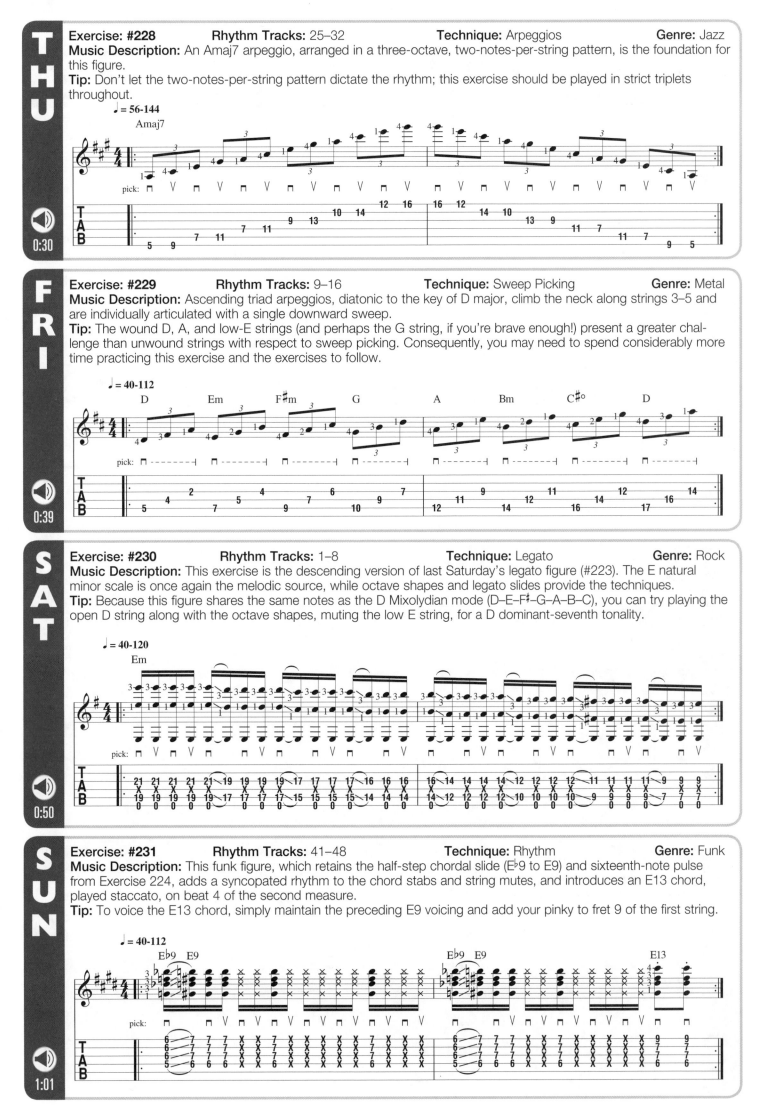

EXERCISE TRACK 34

MON

Exercise: #232   **Rhythm Tracks:** 9–16   **Technique:** Alternate Picking   **Genre:** Metal
Music Description: The arpeggios from last week (#225) have been extended to include the third string. These ascending patterns start on the chords fifth degree (e.g., A for the D chord, E for the A chord) and end on the fifth degree, one octave higher.
Tip: Remember, this is an alternate-picking exercise, so avoid the temptation to use a downwards sweep for the first three notes of each beat.

0:00

TUE

Exercise: #233   **Rhythm Tracks:** 9–16   **Technique:** String Skipping   **Genre:** Metal
Music Description: Similar to Exercise 226 from last week, this figure also utilizes the C major/A minor scale, only in descending fashion.
Tip: Because of their thickness, wound strings are much harder to pick than unwound strings. Therefore, don't get discouraged if you need to spend more time practicing this exercise than the ones played exclusively on strings 1–3.

0:11

WED

Exercise: #234   **Rhythm Tracks:** 33–40   **Technique:** String Bending   **Genre:** Country
Music Description: In measures 1 and 2, alternating half- and whole-step bends on string 1 target the same pitch, E, before a double-stop slide resolves to the root, C, in measure 3.
Tip: For the first-string bends, use your ear to guide you to the target pitch, E, rather than focusing all of your attention on the distances of each bend.

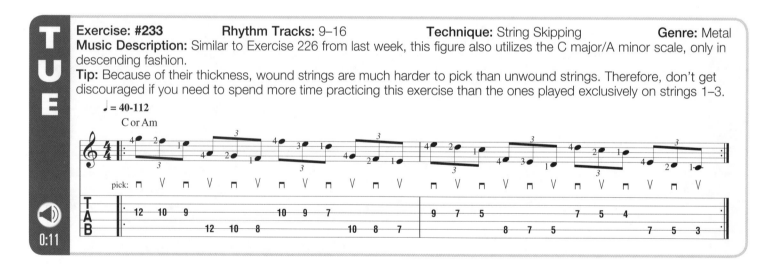

0:22

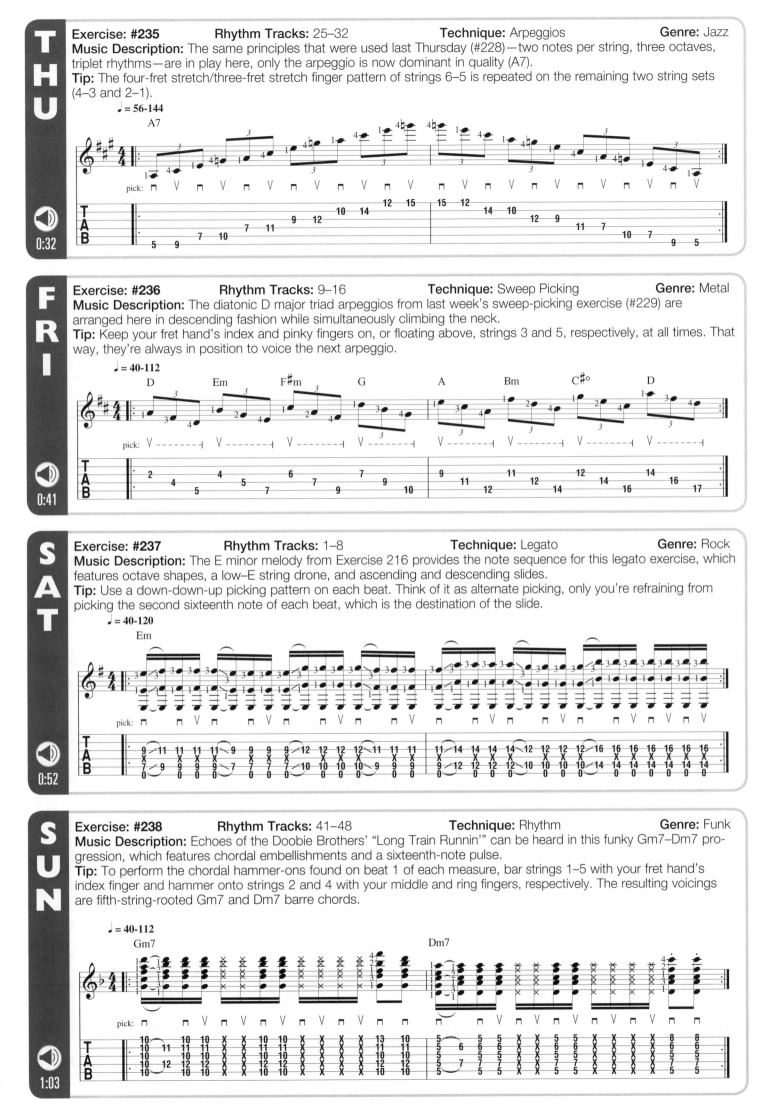

THU

🔊 0:32

Exercise: #235   **Rhythm Tracks:** 25–32   **Technique:** Arpeggios   **Genre:** Jazz
Music Description: The same principles that were used last Thursday (#228)—two notes per string, three octaves, triplet rhythms—are in play here, only the arpeggio is now dominant in quality (A7).
Tip: The four-fret stretch/three-fret stretch finger pattern of strings 6–5 is repeated on the remaining two string sets (4–3 and 2–1).

♩ = 56-144

A7

FRI

🔊 0:41

Exercise: #236   **Rhythm Tracks:** 9–16   **Technique:** Sweep Picking   **Genre:** Metal
Music Description: The diatonic D major triad arpeggios from last week's sweep-picking exercise (#229) are arranged here in descending fashion while simultaneously climbing the neck.
Tip: Keep your fret hand's index and pinky fingers on, or floating above, strings 3 and 5, respectively, at all times. That way, they're always in position to voice the next arpeggio.

♩ = 40-112

D   Em   F#m   G   A   Bm   C#°   D

SAT

🔊 0:52

Exercise: #237   **Rhythm Tracks:** 1–8   **Technique:** Legato   **Genre:** Rock
Music Description: The E minor melody from Exercise 216 provides the note sequence for this legato exercise, which features octave shapes, a low–E string drone, and ascending and descending slides.
Tip: Use a down-down-up picking pattern on each beat. Think of it as alternate picking, only you're refraining from picking the second sixteenth note of each beat, which is the destination of the slide.

♩ = 40-120

Em

SUN

🔊 1:03

Exercise: #238   **Rhythm Tracks:** 41–48   **Technique:** Rhythm   **Genre:** Funk
Music Description: Echoes of the Doobie Brothers' "Long Train Runnin'" can be heard in this funky Gm7–Dm7 progression, which features chordal embellishments and a sixteenth-note pulse.
Tip: To perform the chordal hammer-ons found on beat 1 of each measure, bar strings 1–5 with your fret hand's index finger and hammer onto strings 2 and 4 with your middle and ring fingers, respectively. The resulting voicings are fifth-string-rooted Gm7 and Dm7 barre chords.

♩ = 40-112

Gm7   Dm7

73

EXERCISE TRACK 35

MON

Exercise: #239 **Rhythm Tracks:** 9–16 **Technique:** Alternate Picking **Genre:** Metal
Music Description: A mirror image of last Monday's exercise (#232), the four-note arpeggios now descend strings 1–3 as you work through the major and minor chords in the key of D.
Tip: Similar to last week, avoid the temptation to employ an upward sweep to play the last three notes of each beat.

0:00

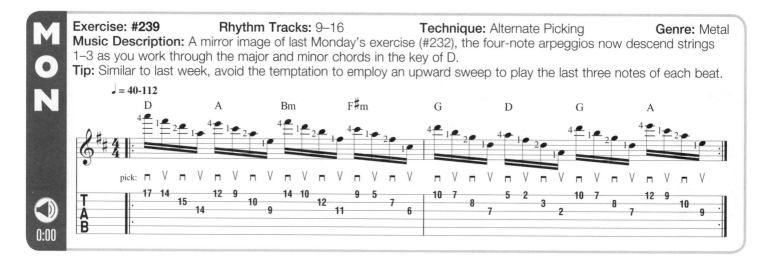

TUE

Exercise: #240 **Rhythm Tracks:** 9–16 **Technique:** String Skipping **Genre:** Metal
Music Description: This string-skipping figure is similar to Exercise 226 from Week 33, only the C major/A minor scale is arranged in descending three-note patterns that gradually make their way up the two strings.
Tip: Try to use your ring finger to fret the note at the eighth fret of string 5. That way, your pinky has a shorter distance to travel to play the first note of string 3.

0:11

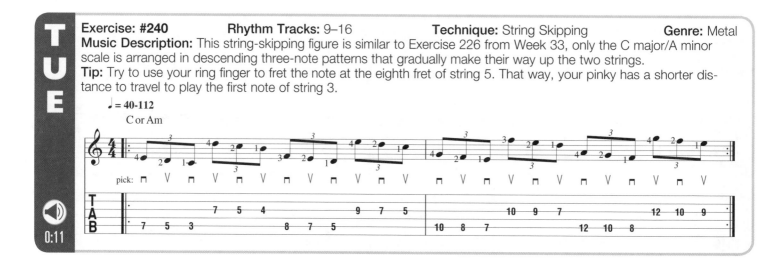

WED

Exercise: #241 **Rhythm Tracks:** 33–40 **Technique:** String Bending **Genre:** Country
Music Description: Half-step bends and pre-bends are incorporated into a descending D Mixolydian (D–E–F#–G–A–B–C) phrase.
Tip: In measure 3, bend the fourth string upwards (towards the ceiling) with your index finger.

0:22

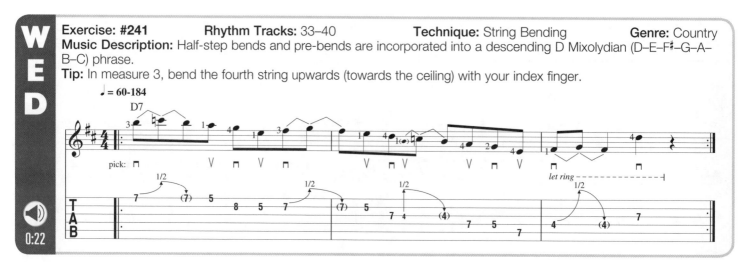

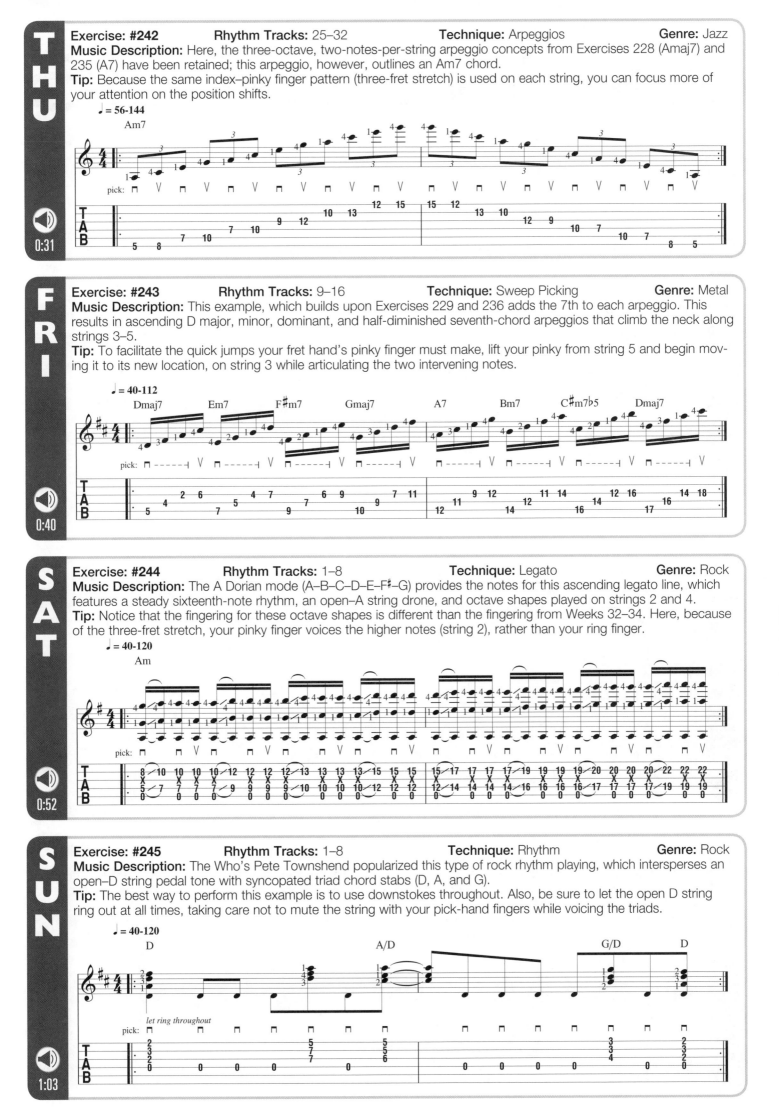

THU

Exercise: **#242**   Rhythm Tracks: 25–32   Technique: Arpeggios   Genre: Jazz

Music Description: Here, the three-octave, two-notes-per-string arpeggio concepts from Exercises 228 (Amaj7) and 235 (A7) have been retained; this arpeggio, however, outlines an Am7 chord.

Tip: Because the same index–pinky finger pattern (three-fret stretch) is used on each string, you can focus more of your attention on the position shifts.

0:31

FRI

Exercise: **#243**   Rhythm Tracks: 9–16   Technique: Sweep Picking   Genre: Metal

Music Description: This example, which builds upon Exercises 229 and 236 adds the 7th to each arpeggio. This results in ascending D major, minor, dominant, and half-diminished seventh-chord arpeggios that climb the neck along strings 3–5.

Tip: To facilitate the quick jumps your fret hand's pinky finger must make, lift your pinky from string 5 and begin moving it to its new location, on string 3 while articulating the two intervening notes.

0:40

SAT

Exercise: **#244**   Rhythm Tracks: 1–8   Technique: Legato   Genre: Rock

Music Description: The A Dorian mode (A–B–C–D–E–F#–G) provides the notes for this ascending legato line, which features a steady sixteenth-note rhythm, an open–A string drone, and octave shapes played on strings 2 and 4.

Tip: Notice that the fingering for these octave shapes is different than the fingering from Weeks 32–34. Here, because of the three-fret stretch, your pinky finger voices the higher notes (string 2), rather than your ring finger.

0:52

SUN

Exercise: **#245**   Rhythm Tracks: 1–8   Technique: Rhythm   Genre: Rock

Music Description: The Who's Pete Townshend popularized this type of rock rhythm playing, which intersperses an open–D string pedal tone with syncopated triad chord stabs (D, A, and G).

Tip: The best way to perform this example is to use downstokes throughout. Also, be sure to let the open D string ring out at all times, taking care not to mute the string with your pick-hand fingers while voicing the triads.

1:03

EXERCISE TRACK 36

MON

Exercise: #246 **Rhythm Tracks:** 9–16 **Technique:** Alternate Picking **Genre:** Metal

Music Description: The alternate-picking exercises of the previous two weeks (#232 and #239) have been combined to form an alternating ascending/descending arpeggio pattern.

Tip: Let your pinky and index fingers guide you along strings 1 and 3, respectively, as you jump from one arpeggio pattern to the next.

0:00

TUE

Exercise: #247 **Rhythm Tracks:** 9–16 **Technique:** String Skipping **Genre:** Metal

Music Description: Like Exercise 233 from Week 34, the pattern in this figure moves horizontally down the neck. This time, however, the three-note groupings ascend their respective strings.

Tip: If these string-skipping exercises are giving you trouble, try switching to your neck pickup. Sometimes a new tone can inspire your playing.

0:12

WED

Exercise: #248 **Rhythm Tracks:** 33–40 **Technique:** String Bending **Genre:** Country

Music Description: In this descending pedal steel–style phrase, whole- and half-step bends and pre-bends help navigate a D–A–D (I–V–I) progression.

Tip: Pull the fifth string downwards (towards the floor) to perform the last bend, reinforcing your ring finger with your middle and index fingers.

0:23

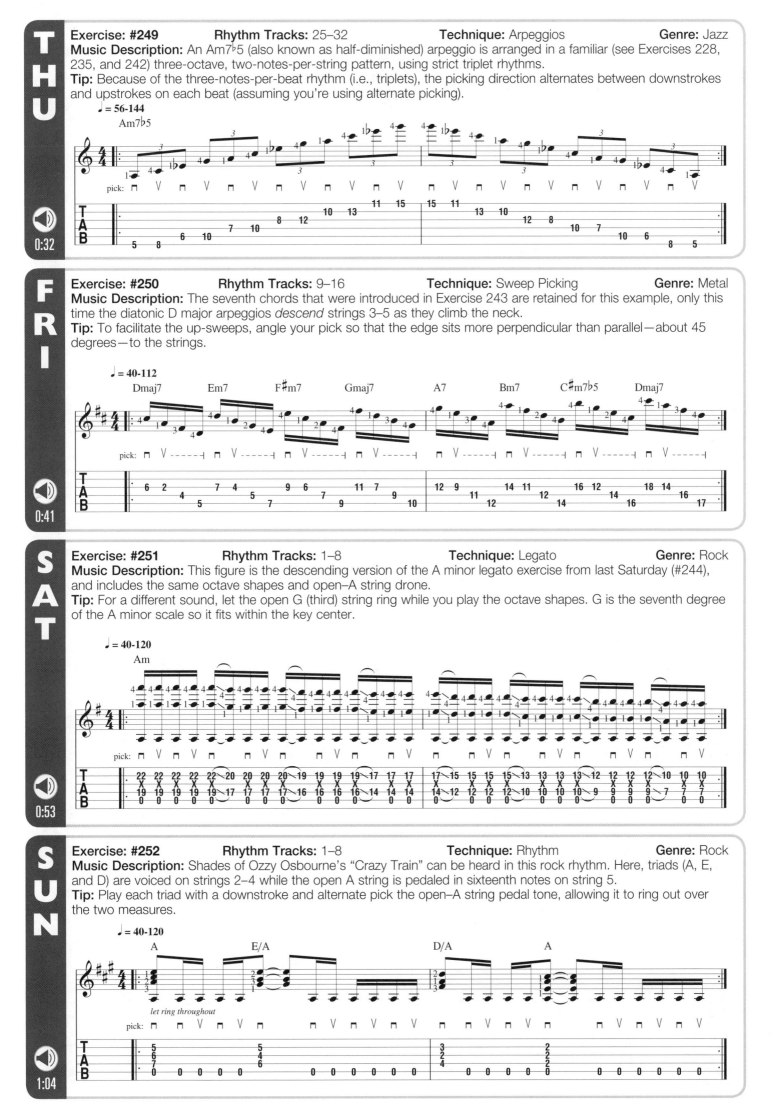

THU

0:32

Exercise: #249   **Rhythm Tracks:** 25–32   **Technique:** Arpeggios   **Genre:** Jazz
Music Description: An Am7♭5 (also known as half-diminished) arpeggio is arranged in a familiar (see Exercises 228, 235, and 242) three-octave, two-notes-per-string pattern, using strict triplet rhythms.
Tip: Because of the three-notes-per-beat rhythm (i.e., triplets), the picking direction alternates between downstrokes and upstrokes on each beat (assuming you're using alternate picking).

FRI

0:41

Exercise: #250   **Rhythm Tracks:** 9–16   **Technique:** Sweep Picking   **Genre:** Metal
Music Description: The seventh chords that were introduced in Exercise 243 are retained for this example, only this time the diatonic D major arpeggios *descend* strings 3–5 as they climb the neck.
Tip: To facilitate the up-sweeps, angle your pick so that the edge sits more perpendicular than parallel—about 45 degrees—to the strings.

SAT

0:53

Exercise: #251   **Rhythm Tracks:** 1–8   **Technique:** Legato   **Genre:** Rock
Music Description: This figure is the descending version of the A minor legato exercise from last Saturday (#244), and includes the same octave shapes and open–A string drone.
Tip: For a different sound, let the open G (third) string ring while you play the octave shapes. G is the seventh degree of the A minor scale so it fits within the key center.

SUN

1:04

Exercise: #252   **Rhythm Tracks:** 1–8   **Technique:** Rhythm   **Genre:** Rock
Music Description: Shades of Ozzy Osbourne's "Crazy Train" can be heard in this rock rhythm. Here, triads (A, E, and D) are voiced on strings 2–4 while the open A string is pedaled in sixteenth notes on string 5.
Tip: Play each triad with a downstroke and alternate pick the open–A string pedal tone, allowing it to ring out over the two measures.

EXERCISE TRACK 37

MON

Exercise: #253   **Rhythm Tracks:** 9–16   **Technique:** Alternate Picking   **Genre:** Metal
Music Description: This is a "pedal-tone" lick, so named because the high E note (first string, 12th fret) is repeated, or "pedaled," between the descending scale tones; in this case, the E harmonic minor scale.
Tip: Attack the pickup note (E; third string, ninth fret) with a downstroke. It will make skipping over string 2 much easier.

0:00

TUE

Exercise: #254   **Rhythm Tracks:** 9–16   **Technique:** String Skipping   **Genre:** Metal
Music Description: This figure is an extension of the C major/A minor string-skipping exercises of the past several weeks, only the three-notes-per-string patterns have shifted from strings 3 and 5 to strings 4 and 6.
Tip: Once you've played through all eight sets of the exercise beginning with a downstroke, try starting it with an upstroke.

0:11

WED

Exercise: #255   **Rhythm Tracks:** 33–40   **Technique:** String Bending   **Genre:** Country
Music Description: A repeated pattern, featuring a fourth-string pre-bend, moves down the neck, from twelfth position to tenth position to fifth position, to nail the D–C–G (V–IV–I) progression.
Tip: Be sure to arch your bending (middle) finger for the last bend so as to not mute the open strings, which should ring in unison with the bent note.

0:22

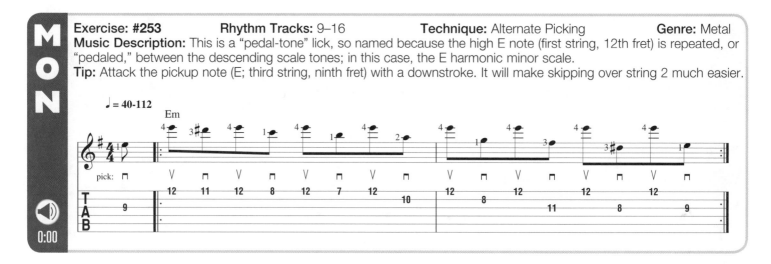

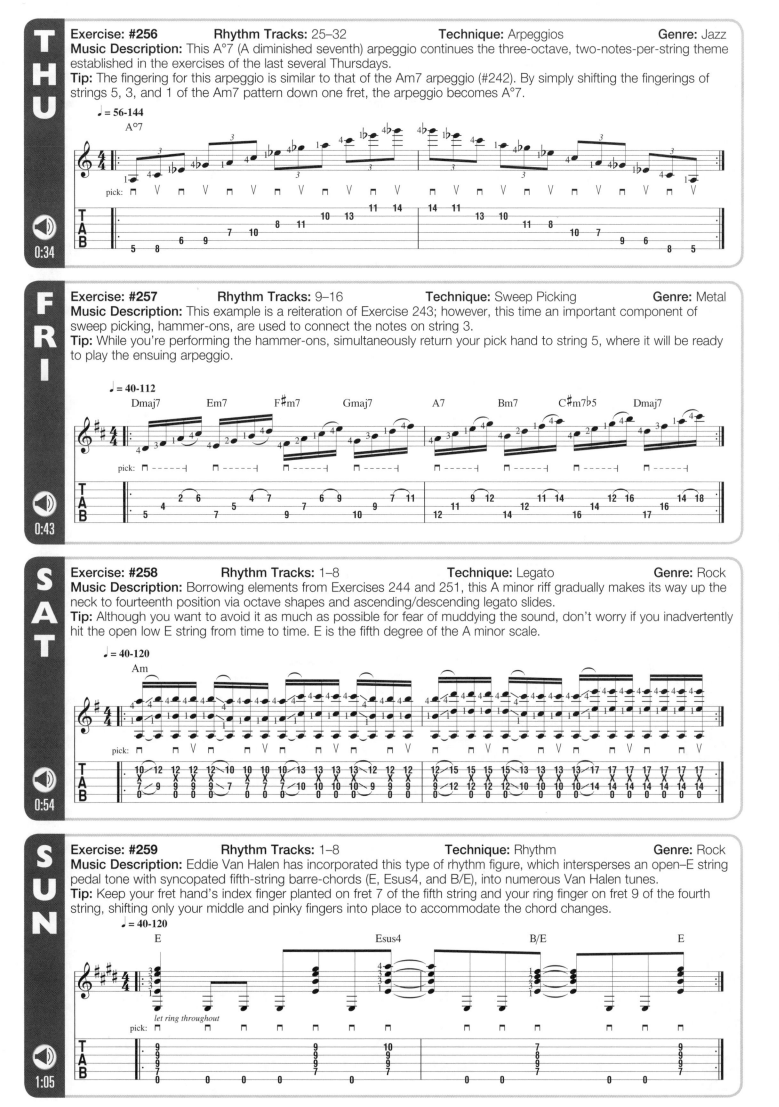

THU

Exercise: #256   **Rhythm Tracks:** 25–32   **Technique:** Arpeggios   **Genre:** Jazz
Music Description: This A°7 (A diminished seventh) arpeggio continues the three-octave, two-notes-per-string theme established in the exercises of the last several Thursdays.
Tip: The fingering for this arpeggio is similar to that of the Am7 arpeggio (#242). By simply shifting the fingerings of strings 5, 3, and 1 of the Am7 pattern down one fret, the arpeggio becomes A°7.

0:34

FRI

Exercise: #257   **Rhythm Tracks:** 9–16   **Technique:** Sweep Picking   **Genre:** Metal
Music Description: This example is a reiteration of Exercise 243; however, this time an important component of sweep picking, hammer-ons, are used to connect the notes on string 3.
Tip: While you're performing the hammer-ons, simultaneously return your pick hand to string 5, where it will be ready to play the ensuing arpeggio.

0:43

SAT

Exercise: #258   **Rhythm Tracks:** 1–8   **Technique:** Legato   **Genre:** Rock
Music Description: Borrowing elements from Exercises 244 and 251, this A minor riff gradually makes its way up the neck to fourteenth position via octave shapes and ascending/descending legato slides.
Tip: Although you want to avoid it as much as possible for fear of muddying the sound, don't worry if you inadvertently hit the open low E string from time to time. E is the fifth degree of the A minor scale.

0:54

SUN

Exercise: #259   **Rhythm Tracks:** 1–8   **Technique:** Rhythm   **Genre:** Rock
Music Description: Eddie Van Halen has incorporated this type of rhythm figure, which intersperses an open–E string pedal tone with syncopated fifth-string barre-chords (E, Esus4, and B/E), into numerous Van Halen tunes.
Tip: Keep your fret hand's index finger planted on fret 7 of the fifth string and your ring finger on fret 9 of the fourth string, shifting only your middle and pinky fingers into place to accommodate the chord changes.

1:05

EXERCISE TRACK 38

MON

Exercise: #260   **Rhythm Tracks:** 9–16   **Technique:** Alternate Picking   **Genre:** Metal
Music Description: This pedal-tone lick differs from last week's lick in two ways. First, a three-note pattern (instead of one note) constitutes the pedal tone. Second, the pedal tone is located on string 3 rather than string 1, where the E harmonic minor scale starts its descent.
Tip: Use a down-up-down-up picking pattern for each beat, attacking each descending scale tone with an upstroke.

0:00

TUE

Exercise: #261   **Rhythm Tracks:** 9–16   **Technique:** String Skipping   **Genre:** Metal
Music Description: Last Tuesday's exercise (#254) utilized the C major/A minor scale to ascend strings 4 and 6 in three-note groupings, skipping over string 5. Here, the pattern descends those two strings in the same manner.
Tip: By now, you may be tired of hearing the same old scale. Feel free to substitute different major or minor scales or modes in place of the C major/A minor scale used here.

0:11

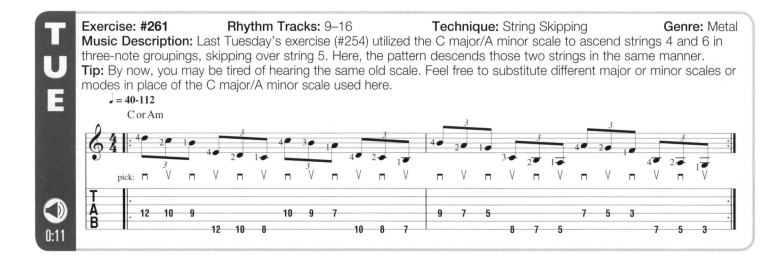

WED

Exercise: #262   **Rhythm Tracks:** 33–40   **Technique:** String Bending   **Genre:** Country
Music Description: This chordal-bending exercise features whole-step bends and releases on string 3 and fixed notes played simultaneously on strings 4 and 5, all of which outline a descending D–C–G (V–IV–I) progression.
Tip: The bends should be performed by pulling the third string downwards (toward the floor) with your index finger.

0:22

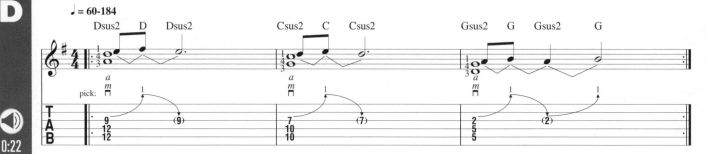

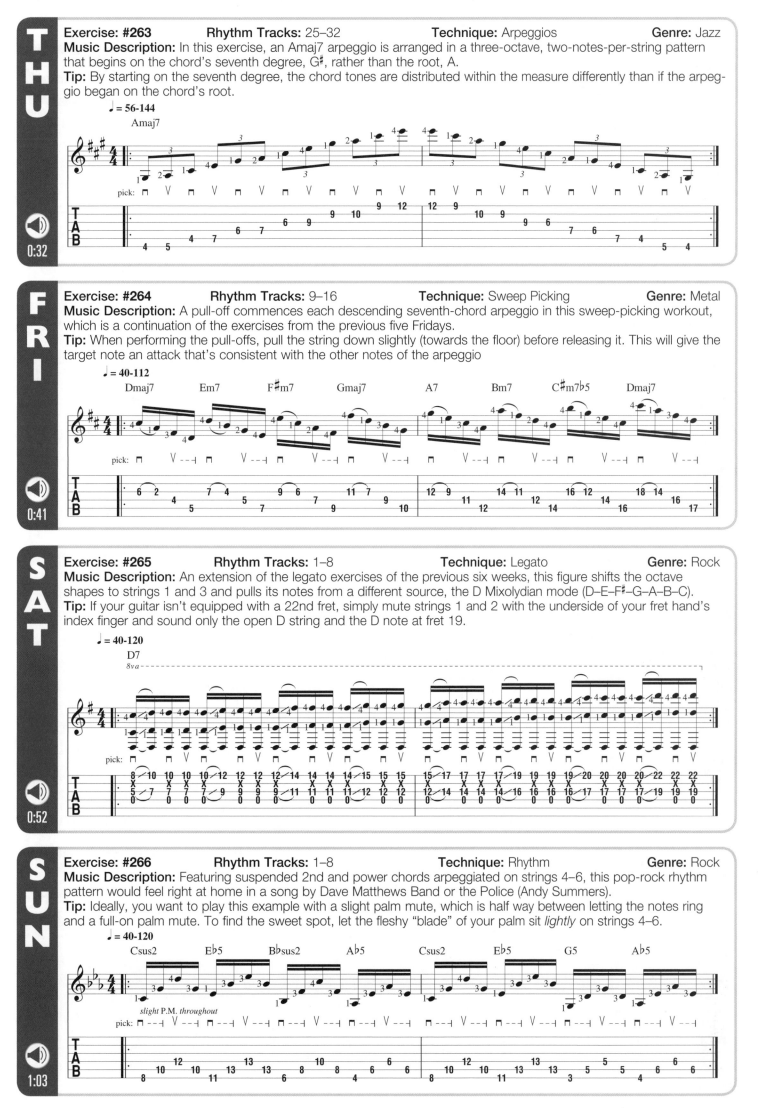

THU

0:32

Exercise: #263   **Rhythm Tracks:** 25–32   **Technique:** Arpeggios   **Genre:** Jazz

Music Description: In this exercise, an Amaj7 arpeggio is arranged in a three-octave, two-notes-per-string pattern that begins on the chord's seventh degree, G♯, rather than the root, A.

Tip: By starting on the seventh degree, the chord tones are distributed within the measure differently than if the arpeggio began on the chord's root.

FRI

0:41

Exercise: #264   **Rhythm Tracks:** 9–16   **Technique:** Sweep Picking   **Genre:** Metal

Music Description: A pull-off commences each descending seventh-chord arpeggio in this sweep-picking workout, which is a continuation of the exercises from the previous five Fridays.

Tip: When performing the pull-offs, pull the string down slightly (towards the floor) before releasing it. This will give the target note an attack that's consistent with the other notes of the arpeggio

SAT

0:52

Exercise: #265   **Rhythm Tracks:** 1–8   **Technique:** Legato   **Genre:** Rock

Music Description: An extension of the legato exercises of the previous six weeks, this figure shifts the octave shapes to strings 1 and 3 and pulls its notes from a different source, the D Mixolydian mode (D–E–F♯–G–A–B–C).

Tip: If your guitar isn't equipped with a 22nd fret, simply mute strings 1 and 2 with the underside of your fret hand's index finger and sound only the open D string and the D note at fret 19.

SUN

1:03

Exercise: #266   **Rhythm Tracks:** 1–8   **Technique:** Rhythm   **Genre:** Rock

Music Description: Featuring suspended 2nd and power chords arpeggiated on strings 4–6, this pop-rock rhythm pattern would feel right at home in a song by Dave Matthews Band or the Police (Andy Summers).

Tip: Ideally, you want to play this example with a slight palm mute, which is half way between letting the notes ring and a full-on palm mute. To find the sweet spot, let the fleshy "blade" of your palm sit *lightly* on strings 4–6.

GUITAR AEROBICS

WEEK 39

EXERCISE TRACK 39

MON

Exercise: #267   **Rhythm Tracks:** 9–16   **Technique:** Alternate Picking   **Genre:** Metal

Music Description: This lick, inspired by alternate picking–pro Paul Gilbert, is a clever three-notes-per-string arrangement of the A blues scale (A–C–D–E♭–E–G), capped off by a whole-step bend to the root, A.

Tip: Pay close attention to the triplet rhythm, which causes the picking direction to alternate between upstrokes and downstrokes on each downbeat.

0:00

TUE

Exercise: #268   **Rhythm Tracks:** 9–16   **Technique:** String Skipping   **Genre:** Metal

Music Description: The string-skipping concept from Week 37 (#254) is in play here; however, the order of notes on the two strings has been reversed and is now descending.

Tip: Instead of alternate picking the entire passage, try picking only the first note of each three-note grouping and using pull-offs to articulate the remaining two notes.

0:11

WED

Exercise: #269   **Rhythm Tracks:** 33–40   **Technique:** String Bending   **Genre:** Country

Music Description: Nonadjacent double-string bends are married to sixth intervals to navigate descending D, C, and G chords.

Tip: It's difficult to maintain intonation when bending both strings a half step, so spend extra time on the bends before attempting to play the entire phrase.

0:22

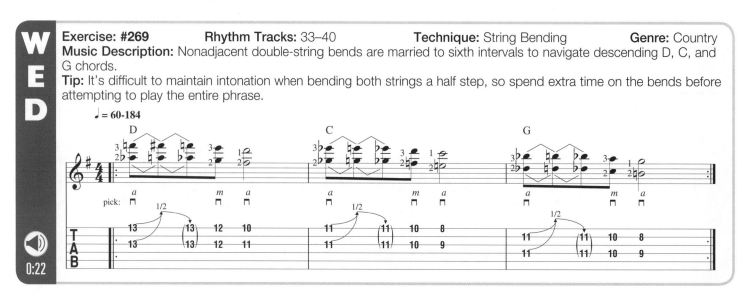

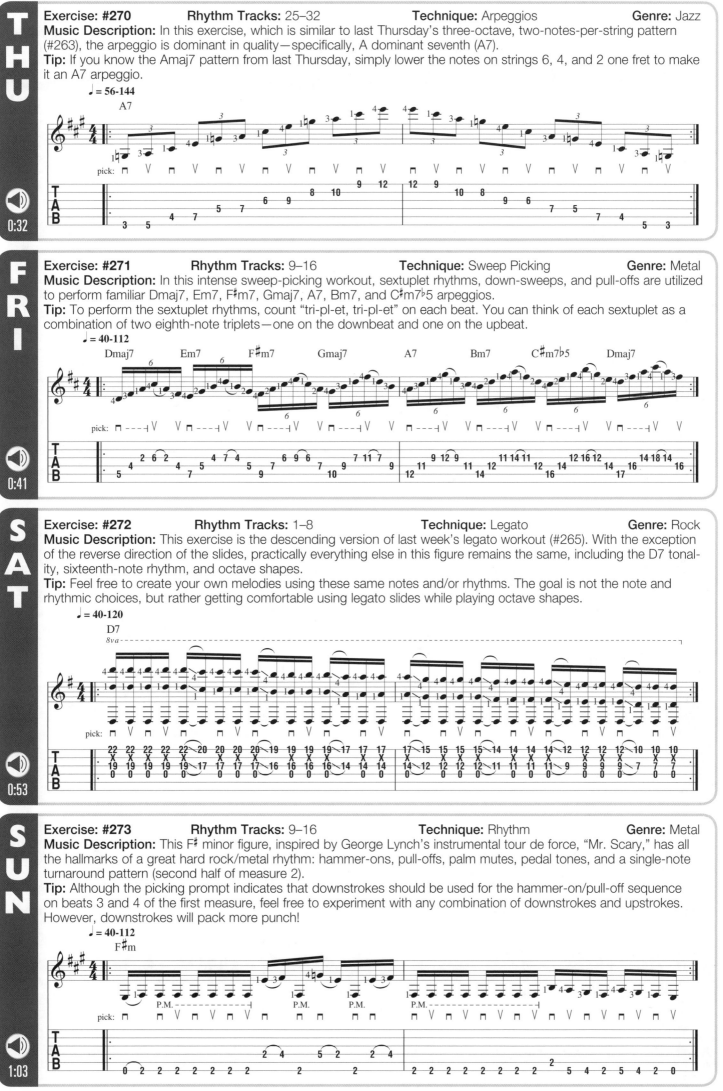

THU

0:32

Exercise: #270 **Rhythm Tracks:** 25–32 **Technique:** Arpeggios **Genre:** Jazz

Music Description: In this exercise, which is similar to last Thursday's three-octave, two-notes-per-string pattern (#263), the arpeggio is dominant in quality—specifically, A dominant seventh (A7).

Tip: If you know the Amaj7 pattern from last Thursday, simply lower the notes on strings 6, 4, and 2 one fret to make it an A7 arpeggio.

FRI

0:41

Exercise: #271 **Rhythm Tracks:** 9–16 **Technique:** Sweep Picking **Genre:** Metal

Music Description: In this intense sweep-picking workout, sextuplet rhythms, down-sweeps, and pull-offs are utilized to perform familiar Dmaj7, Em7, F#m7, Gmaj7, A7, Bm7, and C#m7♭5 arpeggios.

Tip: To perform the sextuplet rhythms, count "tri-pl-et, tri-pl-et" on each beat. You can think of each sextuplet as a combination of two eighth-note triplets—one on the downbeat and one on the upbeat.

SAT

0:53

Exercise: #272 **Rhythm Tracks:** 1–8 **Technique:** Legato **Genre:** Rock

Music Description: This exercise is the descending version of last week's legato workout (#265). With the exception of the reverse direction of the slides, practically everything else in this figure remains the same, including the D7 tonality, sixteenth-note rhythm, and octave shapes.

Tip: Feel free to create your own melodies using these same notes and/or rhythms. The goal is not the note and rhythmic choices, but rather getting comfortable using legato slides while playing octave shapes.

SUN

1:03

Exercise: #273 **Rhythm Tracks:** 9–16 **Technique:** Rhythm **Genre:** Metal

Music Description: This F# minor figure, inspired by George Lynch's instrumental tour de force, "Mr. Scary," has all the hallmarks of a great hard rock/metal rhythm: hammer-ons, pull-offs, palm mutes, pedal tones, and a single-note turnaround pattern (second half of measure 2).

Tip: Although the picking prompt indicates that downstrokes should be used for the hammer-on/pull-off sequence on beats 3 and 4 of the first measure, feel free to experiment with any combination of downstrokes and upstrokes. However, downstrokes will pack more punch!

EXERCISE TRACK 40

MON

Exercise: #274   **Rhythm Tracks:** 9–16   **Technique:** Alternate Picking   **Genre:** Metal

Music Description: This A natural minor scale (A–B–C–D–E–F–G) sequence is built for speed! It's also a good primer on *crosspicking*, or "outside" picking, which involves using alternating downstrokes and upstrokes to pick the "outside" of two adjacent strings.

Tip: While it's perfectly acceptable to commence this pattern with a downstroke, starting it with an upstroke engages the advantageous crosspicking technique.

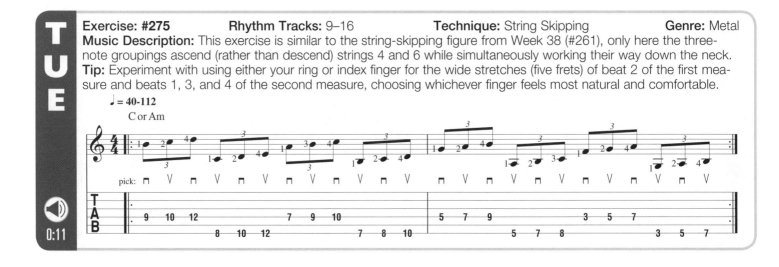

TUE

Exercise: #275   **Rhythm Tracks:** 9–16   **Technique:** String Skipping   **Genre:** Metal

Music Description: This exercise is similar to the string-skipping figure from Week 38 (#261), only here the three-note groupings ascend (rather than descend) strings 4 and 6 while simultaneously working their way down the neck.

Tip: Experiment with using either your ring or index finger for the wide stretches (five frets) of beat 2 of the first measure and beats 1, 3, and 4 of the second measure, choosing whichever finger feels most natural and comfortable.

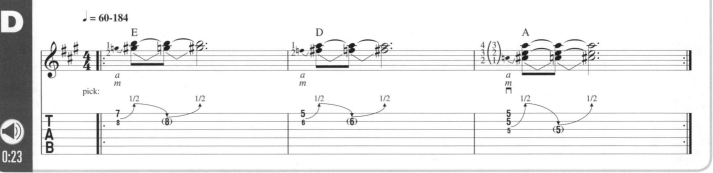

WED

Exercise: #276   **Rhythm Tracks:** 33–40   **Technique:** String Bending   **Genre:** Country

Music Description: E, D, and A chords are outlined with two- (E and D) and three-note (A) oblique bends.

Tip: For the three-note oblique bend, experiment with the two fingerings offered in the notation staff, using whichever is most comfortable.

THU

Exercise: #277   **Rhythm Tracks:** 25–32   **Technique:** Arpeggios   **Genre:** Jazz

Music Description: Once again, the three-octave, two-notes-per-string arpeggio pattern that has been utilized the last several weeks is put into play. Here, the pattern outlines an Am7 chord.

Tip: Don't forget to repeat the pattern's top note, E (twelfth fret, string 1), before starting the descent. Likewise, the lowest note, G (third fret, string 6), is restated on the pattern's repetition.

0:32

FRI

Exercise: #278   **Rhythm Tracks:** 9–16   **Technique:** Sweep Picking   **Genre:** Metal

Music Description: This figure employs the same fingerings found in the sweep-picking exercises from Weeks 33–34; however, here the triad arpeggios are played on strings 4–6, thus changing the key center from D major to A major.

Tip: Use the fleshy underside of your fret hand's index finger to mute strings 1–3, preventing unwanted string noise.

0:41

SAT

Exercise: #279   **Rhythm Tracks:** 1–8   **Technique:** Legato   **Genre:** Rock

Music Description: The D Mixolydian mode, octave shapes on strings 1 and 3, sixteenth-note rhythms, and ascending/descending legato slides, all of which are borrowed from Exercises 265 and 272, are combined here to produce a droning riff reminiscent of some of Richie Sambora's work in Bon Jovi.

Tip: Planting your fret-hand thumb on the back of the neck—rather than draping it over the top of the fretboard—will help keep proper spacing between your index and pinky fingers while you move the octave shapes up and down the neck.

0:53

SUN

Exercise: #280   **Rhythm Tracks:** 9–16   **Technique:** Rhythm   **Genre:** Metal

Music Description: Similar to a riff found in Megadeth's "Peace Sells," this metal passage features the E natural minor scale (E–F#–G–A–B–C–D) arranged in multiple three-note pull-off/hammer-on moves that descend strings 5 and 6, while a low E–string pedal firmly establishes the riff's E minor tonality.

Tip: In metal, it's common for guitarists to use downstrokes exclusively whenever possible. This practice imparts a firm attack to riffs, something alternate picking doesn't provide—but this exercise does!

1:04

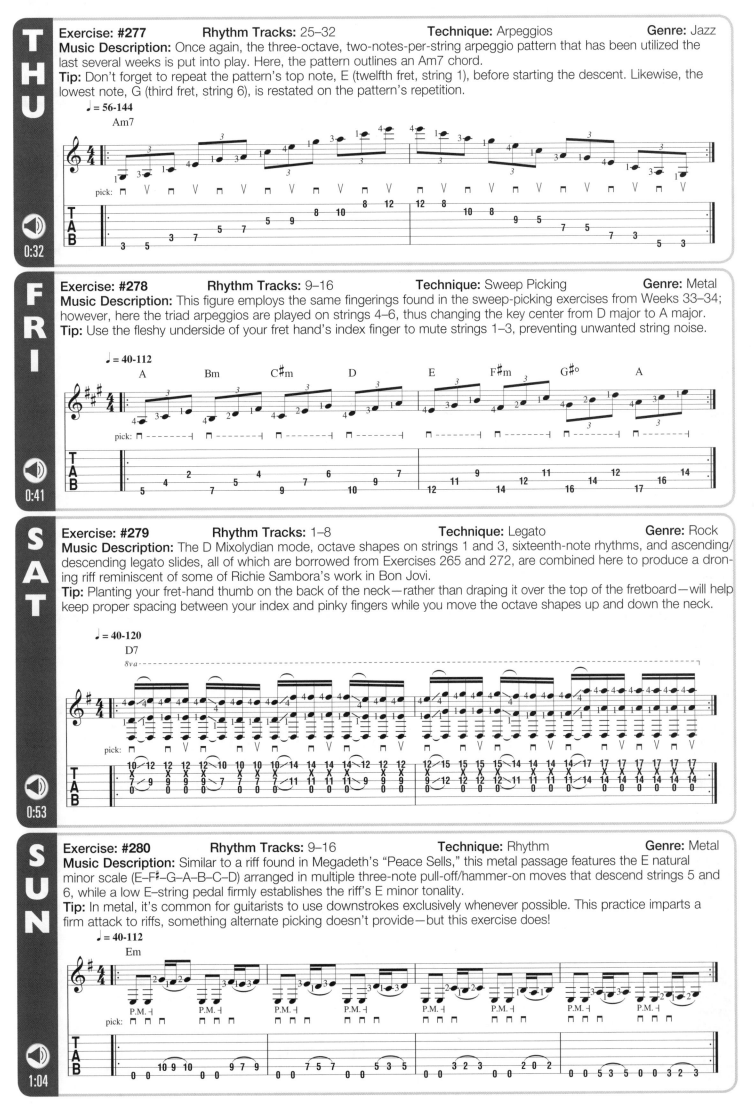

WEEK 41

EXERCISE TRACK 41

MON

Exercise: #281   **Rhythm Tracks:** 9–16   **Technique:** Alternate Picking   **Genre:** Metal
Music Description: The A natural minor scale is also used for this alternate-picking exercise. Here, the scale is arranged in a three-notes-per-string sequence that ascends strings 1 and 2 and is capped with a whole-step bend to the root, A.
Tip: In the picking prompt notated between staves, notice that a downstroke is used to begin each three-note sequence on string 2 and an upstroke starts each sequence on string 1.

0:00

TUE

Exercise: #282   **Rhythm Tracks:** 9–16   **Technique:** String Skipping   **Genre:** Metal
Music Description: Ascending Am, C, G, and Em arpeggios are arranged in a two-bar string-skipping pattern, with each arpeggio spanning four strings and skipping one.
Tip: Each arpeggio uses the same three fingers (index, middle, and pinky), with only a slight adjustment to accommodate the different chord qualities (major or minor).

0:14

WED

Exercise: #283   **Rhythm Tracks:** 33–40   **Technique:** String Bending   **Genre:** Country
Music Description: Double-string pre-bends—with each string bent to a different interval (half and whole steps)—highlight this exercise, which follows an E–D–A progression down the neck.
Tip: The respective tensions of strings 2 and 3 are conducive to simultaneously hitting the half- and whole-step bends; however, it will take considerable practice to achieve perfect intonation of both strings on demand.

0:26

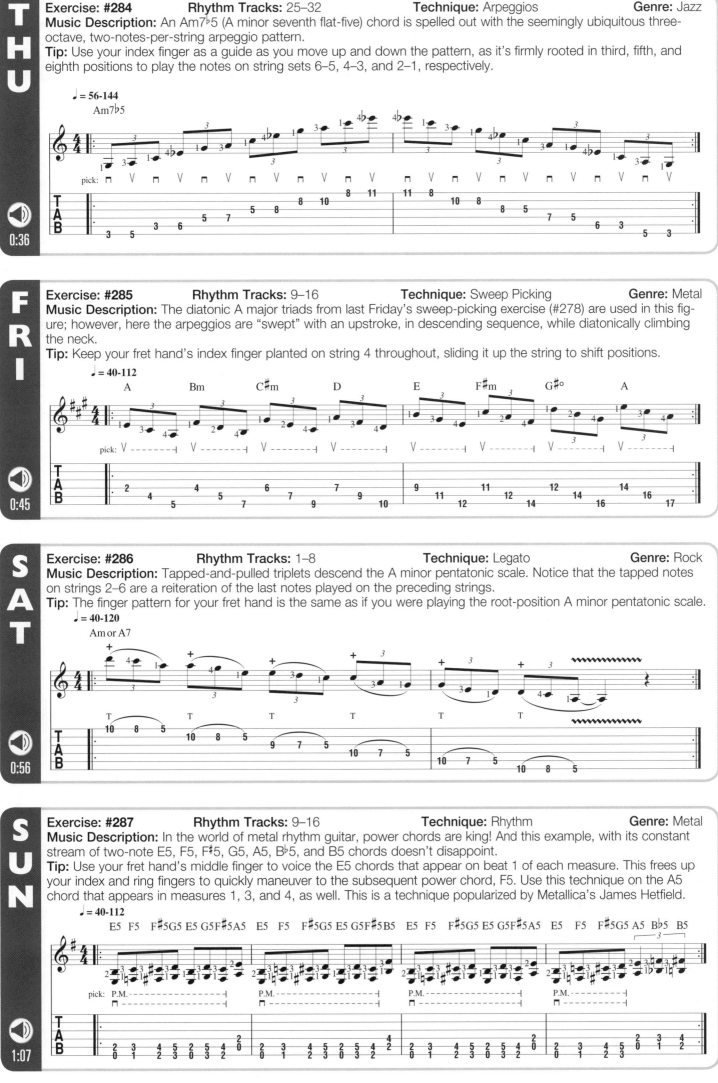

THU

0:36

Exercise: #284　　　**Rhythm Tracks:** 25–32　　　**Technique:** Arpeggios　　　**Genre:** Jazz

Music Description: An Am7♭5 (A minor seventh flat-five) chord is spelled out with the seemingly ubiquitous three-octave, two-notes-per-string arpeggio pattern.

Tip: Use your index finger as a guide as you move up and down the pattern, as it's firmly rooted in third, fifth, and eighth positions to play the notes on string sets 6–5, 4–3, and 2–1, respectively.

FRI

0:45

Exercise: #285　　　**Rhythm Tracks:** 9–16　　　**Technique:** Sweep Picking　　　**Genre:** Metal

Music Description: The diatonic A major triads from last Friday's sweep-picking exercise (#278) are used in this figure; however, here the arpeggios are "swept" with an upstroke, in descending sequence, while diatonically climbing the neck.

Tip: Keep your fret hand's index finger planted on string 4 throughout, sliding it up the string to shift positions.

SAT

0:56

Exercise: #286　　　**Rhythm Tracks:** 1–8　　　**Technique:** Legato　　　**Genre:** Rock

Music Description: Tapped-and-pulled triplets descend the A minor pentatonic scale. Notice that the tapped notes on strings 2–6 are a reiteration of the last notes played on the preceding strings.

Tip: The finger pattern for your fret hand is the same as if you were playing the root-position A minor pentatonic scale.

SUN

1:07

Exercise: #287　　　**Rhythm Tracks:** 9–16　　　**Technique:** Rhythm　　　**Genre:** Metal

Music Description: In the world of metal rhythm guitar, power chords are king! And this example, with its constant stream of two-note E5, F5, F♯5, G5, A5, B♭5, and B5 chords doesn't disappoint.

Tip: Use your fret hand's middle finger to voice the E5 chords that appear on beat 1 of each measure. This frees up your index and ring fingers to quickly maneuver to the subsequent power chord, F5. Use this technique on the A5 chord that appears in measures 1, 3, and 4, as well. This is a technique popularized by Metallica's James Hetfield.

EXERCISE TRACK 42

MON

Exercise: #288   **Rhythm Tracks:** 9–16   **Technique:** Alternate Picking   **Genre:** Metal
Music Description: Similar to last Monday's exercise (#281), this figure also utilizes the A natural minor scale in a three-notes-per-string sequence. This time, however, the pattern begins on string 1 and descends to string 2 before climbing horizontally up the neck.
Tip: As you move up the neck, your pinky should guide your hand to the first note of each new six-note grouping.

0:00

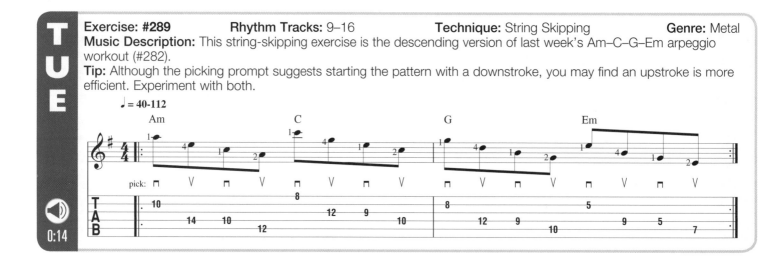

TUE

Exercise: #289   **Rhythm Tracks:** 9–16   **Technique:** String Skipping   **Genre:** Metal
Music Description: This string-skipping exercise is the descending version of last week's Am–C–G–Em arpeggio workout (#282).
Tip: Although the picking prompt suggests starting the pattern with a downstroke, you may find an upstroke is more efficient. Experiment with both.

0:14

WED

Exercise: #290   **Rhythm Tracks:** 33–40   **Technique:** String Bending   **Genre:** Country
Music Description: Played over an A chord, this example combines oblique bends with pick-hand muting to produced a percussive effect commonly known as "chicken pickin'."
Tip: Use the middle finger of your pick hand to mute the third string, which is simultaneously attacked with a downstroke of the pick.

0:25

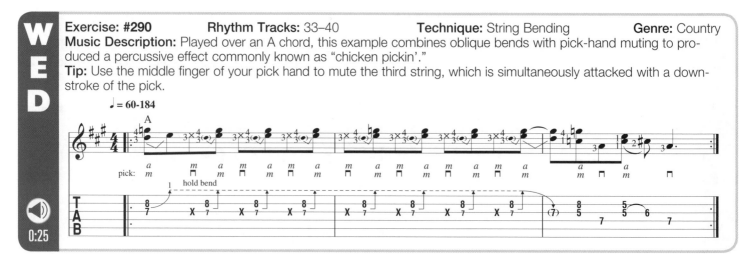

THU

Exercise: #291   **Rhythm Tracks:** 25–32   **Technique:** Arpeggios   **Genre:** Jazz

Music Description: For this next example, an A°7 (A diminished seventh) arpeggio is arranged in a three-octave, two-notes-per-string pattern and played in a strict triplet rhythm throughout.

Tip: The two-notes-per-string index–pinky pattern moves up one fret on each successive string except for string 2, where the pattern moves up two frets.

0:35

FRI

Exercise: #292   **Rhythm Tracks:** 9–16   **Technique:** Sweep Picking   **Genre:** Metal

Music Description: This sweep-picking example borrows the A major triad arpeggios from Exercise 278 and adds a diatonic 7th to each, converting them to major, minor, dominant, or half-diminished seventh chords.

Tip: If jumping your fret hand's pinky from string 6 to string 4 for the major-seventh arpeggios gives you problems, try substituting your ring finger on the low E string.

0:43

SAT

Exercise: #293   **Rhythm Tracks:** 1–8   **Technique:** Legato   **Genre:** Rock

Music Description: In this legato exercise, a tap/pull/hammer sequence is used to ascend the root-position A minor pentatonic scale.

Tip: While you climb the scale, use the "heel" of your pick hand, which should be resting in the vicinity of the seventeenth fret, to mute strings after they've been played, thus preventing unwanted string noise.

0:55

SUN

Exercise: #294   **Rhythm Tracks:** 9–16   **Technique:** Rhythm   **Genre:** Metal

Music Description: Inspired by the doomsday riffs performed by Slayer's guitar duo, Kerry King and Jeff Hanneman, this metallic passage mixes A5, B♭5, B5, and E5 power chords with a haunting tritone melody that's arranged along strings 3–5.

Tip: The first four power chords in this figure are part of a two-beat pickup measure; therefore, the chords are only played once, as a lead-in to the repeated two-measure phrase.

1:05

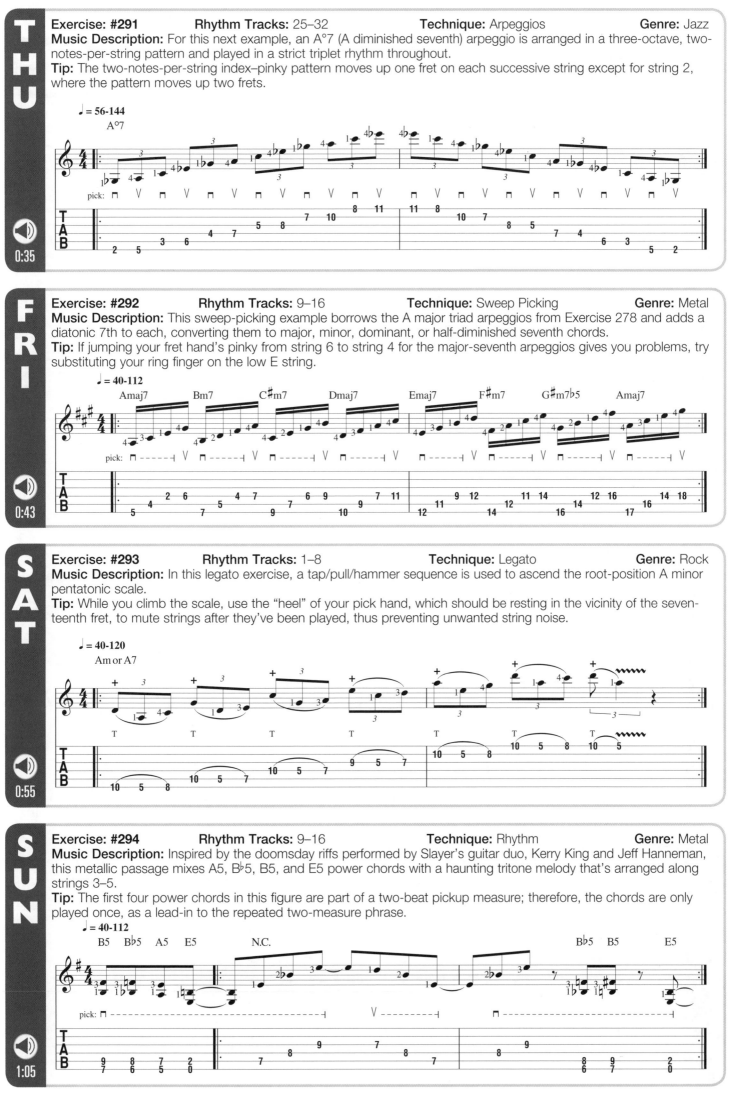

89

WEEK 43

EXERCISE TRACK 43

MON

Exercise: #295   **Rhythm Tracks:** 9–16   **Technique:** Alternate Picking   **Genre:** Metal
Music Description: A variation of the exercises from the previous two Monday's (#281 and #288), this A natural minor scale sequence employs fret-hand slides to facilitate position shifts.
Tip: Unlike the previous two Mondays, straight sixteenth notes are utilized here, so work diligently on not letting the three-against-four feel (three-note groupings against four notes per beat) trip you up.

0:00

TUE

Exercise: #296   **Rhythm Tracks:** 9–16   **Technique:** String Skipping   **Genre:** Metal
Music Description: This exercise builds on the foundation laid by the figures from the previous two Tuesdays (#289 and #282) by adding an additional note on top (major and minor 3rds, depending on the chord quality) and including both ascending and descending forms in each measure.
Tip: For the Am and Em arpeggios, try to use your ring finger (rather than your pinky) to play the highest notes. This will eliminate the need to jump your pinky between strings 2 and 4.

0:11

WED

Exercise: #297   **Rhythm Tracks:** 33–40   **Technique:** String Bending   **Genre:** Country
Music Description: In this example, adjacent- and nonadjacent-string oblique bends and chordal bending are combined for a country workout in the key of A.
Tip: Use hybrid picking—alternating between your pick and middle finger—to perform this lick.

0:29

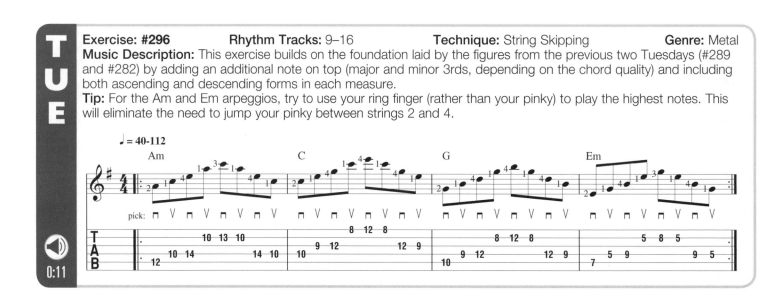

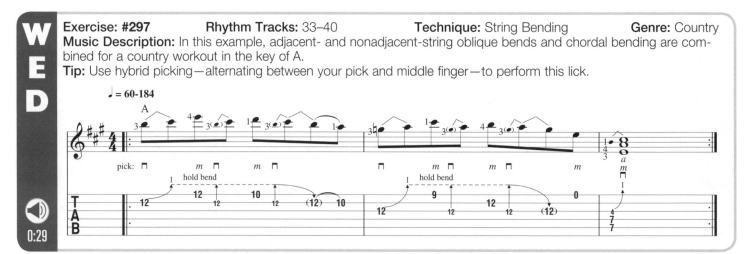

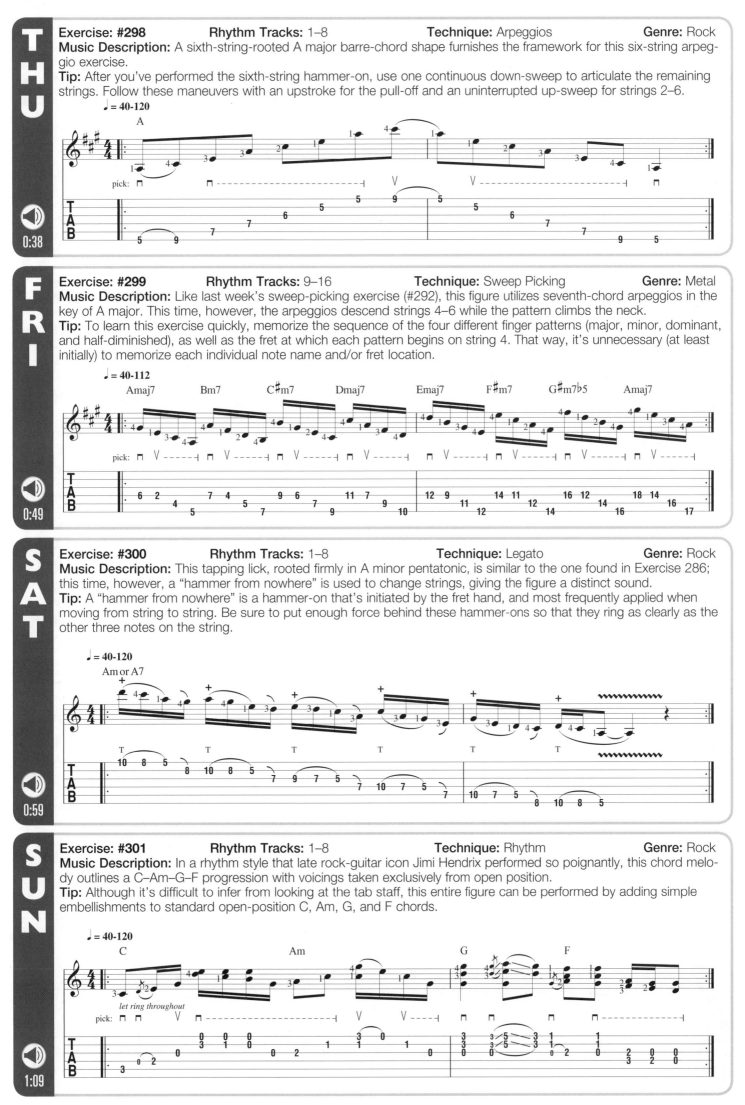

THU

0:38

Exercise: #298 **Rhythm Tracks:** 1–8 **Technique:** Arpeggios **Genre:** Rock

Music Description: A sixth-string-rooted A major barre-chord shape furnishes the framework for this six-string arpeggio exercise.

Tip: After you've performed the sixth-string hammer-on, use one continuous down-sweep to articulate the remaining strings. Follow these maneuvers with an upstroke for the pull-off and an uninterrupted up-sweep for strings 2–6.

FRI

0:49

Exercise: #299 **Rhythm Tracks:** 9–16 **Technique:** Sweep Picking **Genre:** Metal

Music Description: Like last week's sweep-picking exercise (#292), this figure utilizes seventh-chord arpeggios in the key of A major. This time, however, the arpeggios descend strings 4–6 while the pattern climbs the neck.

Tip: To learn this exercise quickly, memorize the sequence of the four different finger patterns (major, minor, dominant, and half-diminished), as well as the fret at which each pattern begins on string 4. That way, it's unnecessary (at least initially) to memorize each individual note name and/or fret location.

SAT

0:59

Exercise: #300 **Rhythm Tracks:** 1–8 **Technique:** Legato **Genre:** Rock

Music Description: This tapping lick, rooted firmly in A minor pentatonic, is similar to the one found in Exercise 286; this time, however, a "hammer from nowhere" is used to change strings, giving the figure a distinct sound.

Tip: A "hammer from nowhere" is a hammer-on that's initiated by the fret hand, and most frequently applied when moving from string to string. Be sure to put enough force behind these hammer-ons so that they ring as clearly as the other three notes on the string.

SUN

1:09

Exercise: #301 **Rhythm Tracks:** 1–8 **Technique:** Rhythm **Genre:** Rock

Music Description: In a rhythm style that late rock-guitar icon Jimi Hendrix performed so poignantly, this chord melody outlines a C–Am–G–F progression with voicings taken exclusively from open position.

Tip: Although it's difficult to infer from looking at the tab staff, this entire figure can be performed by adding simple embellishments to standard open-position C, Am, G, and F chords.

WEEK 44

MON

Exercise: #302   **Rhythm Tracks:** 9–16   **Technique:** Alternate Picking   **Genre:** Metal
Music Description: The same concept as last Monday (#295) is in play here, only the A natural minor scale sequence commences on string 1, descends to string 2, and then climbs horizontally up the neck.
Tip: Don't let the scale sequence dictate your picking pattern; instead, maintain a steady down-up-down-up pattern on each beat throughout.

0:00

TUE

Exercise: #303   **Rhythm Tracks:** 9–16   **Technique:** String Skipping   **Genre:** Metal
Music Description: This string-skipping exercise maintains the same Am–C–G–Em arpeggio sequence from last Tuesday (#296), only the notes in each measure follow a descending-ascending (rather than ascending-descending) pattern.
Tip: To seamlessly transition from the G arpeggio to the Em arpeggio—and the subsequent notes that occur at the eighth fret of string 2—quickly shift from your index finger to your ring finger.

0:11

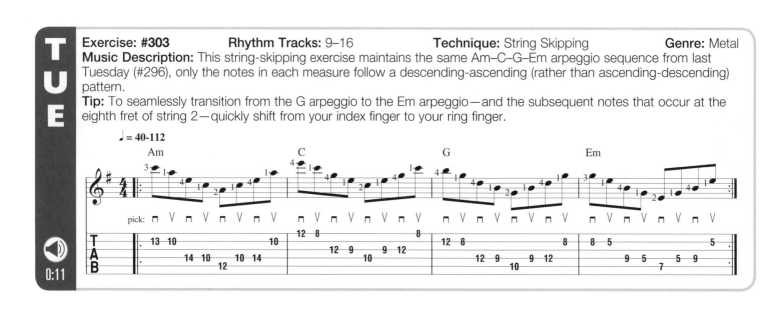

WED

Exercise: #304   **Rhythm Tracks:** 33–40   **Technique:** String Bending   **Genre:** Country
Music Description: Three-string oblique bends (one bent note and two fixed notes) are utilized to outline the E–D–A (V–IV–I) progression.
Tip: Use your ring finger, middle finger, and pick to play the notes on strings 1, 2, and 3, respectively.

0:29

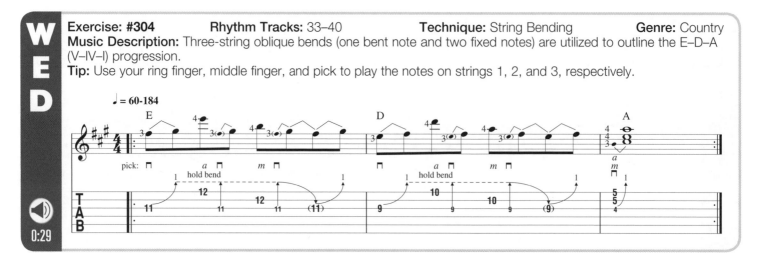

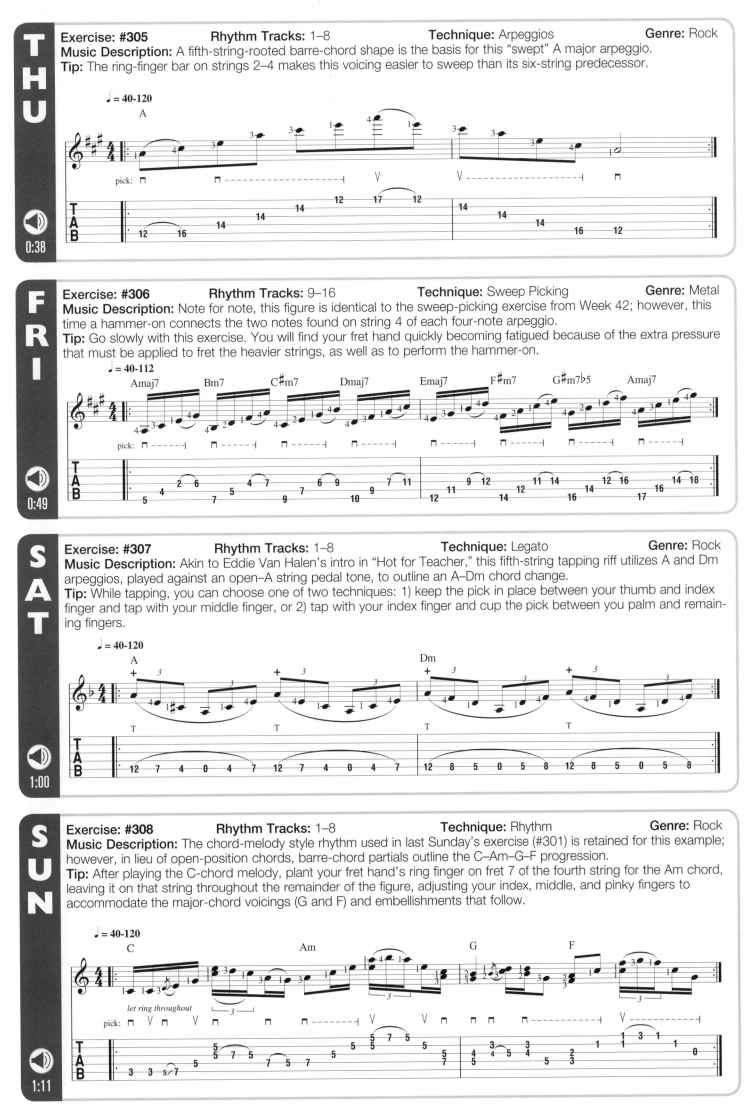

THU

Exercise: #305   **Rhythm Tracks:** 1–8   **Technique:** Arpeggios   **Genre:** Rock
Music Description: A fifth-string-rooted barre-chord shape is the basis for this "swept" A major arpeggio.
Tip: The ring-finger bar on strings 2–4 makes this voicing easier to sweep than its six-string predecessor.

0:38

FRI

Exercise: #306   **Rhythm Tracks:** 9–16   **Technique:** Sweep Picking   **Genre:** Metal
Music Description: Note for note, this figure is identical to the sweep-picking exercise from Week 42; however, this time a hammer-on connects the two notes found on string 4 of each four-note arpeggio.
Tip: Go slowly with this exercise. You will find your fret hand quickly becoming fatigued because of the extra pressure that must be applied to fret the heavier strings, as well as to perform the hammer-on.

0:49

SAT

Exercise: #307   **Rhythm Tracks:** 1–8   **Technique:** Legato   **Genre:** Rock
Music Description: Akin to Eddie Van Halen's intro in "Hot for Teacher," this fifth-string tapping riff utilizes A and Dm arpeggios, played against an open–A string pedal tone, to outline an A–Dm chord change.
Tip: While tapping, you can choose one of two techniques: 1) keep the pick in place between your thumb and index finger and tap with your middle finger, or 2) tap with your index finger and cup the pick between you palm and remaining fingers.

1:00

SUN

Exercise: #308   **Rhythm Tracks:** 1–8   **Technique:** Rhythm   **Genre:** Rock
Music Description: The chord-melody style rhythm used in last Sunday's exercise (#301) is retained for this example; however, in lieu of open-position chords, barre-chord partials outline the C–Am–G–F progression.
Tip: After playing the C-chord melody, plant your fret hand's ring finger on fret 7 of the fourth string for the Am chord, leaving it on that string throughout the remainder of the figure, adjusting your index, middle, and pinky fingers to accommodate the major-chord voicings (G and F) and embellishments that follow.

1:11

93

EXERCISE TRACK 45

MON

Exercise: #309   **Rhythm Tracks:** 9–16   **Technique:** Alternate Picking   **Genre:** Metal

Music Description: This exercise is a straightforward ascension of a (nearly) three-octave A harmonic minor scale, capped with resolution to the root note, A, on string 2.

Tip: The four-note groupings that occur on strings 2 and 4 are tricky, so spend extra time getting those index-finger slides down pat before playing the entire exercise up to speed.

0:00

TUE

Exercise: #310   **Rhythm Tracks:** 25–32   **Technique:** String Skipping   **Genre:** Jazz

Music Description: This snaky bebop line is played over a Gmaj7 chord and features multiple single-string skips as it descends the neck vertically.

Tip: Remember, this is a jazz line, so swing the eighth notes (i.e., play the first eight note of each beat slightly longer than the second).

0:11

WED

Exercise: #311   **Rhythm Tracks:** 33–40   **Technique:** String Bending   **Genre:** Country

Music Description: A new technique is introduced in this figure: bending behind the nut. Here, the E chord in the second measure is outlined with a combination of open first and second strings (E and B) and the open third string raised a half step (to G#) by bending behind the nut.

Tip: You'll need a guitar without a locking nut, such as a Fender Telecaster or Gibson Les Paul, to perform behind-the-nut bends.

0:20

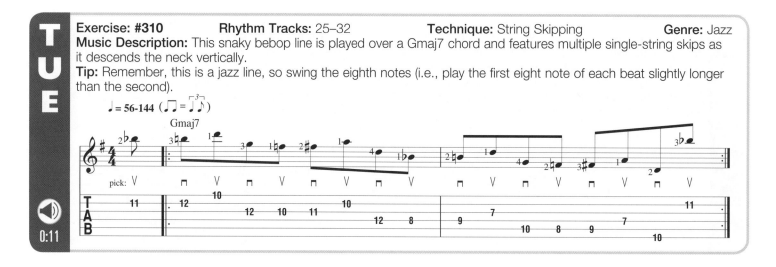

THU

Exercise: #312   **Rhythm Tracks:** 1–8   **Technique:** Arpeggios   **Genre:** Rock

Music Description: This sweep-picking pattern is similar to Exercise 298, only this time the arpeggio is minor (Am) in quality.

Tip: The trick to fretting the ring-finger bar is to "roll" the finger—from the tip to the first knuckle—over strings 5 and 4.

0:28

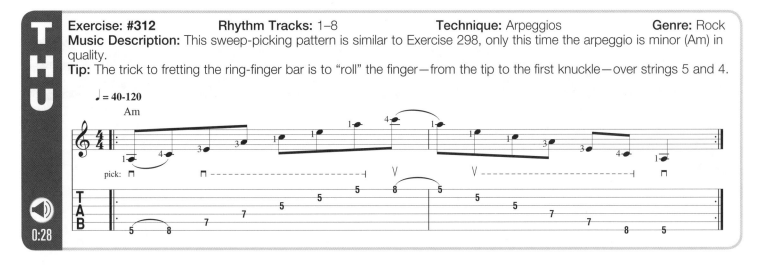

FRI

Exercise: #313   **Rhythm Tracks:** 9–16   **Technique:** Sweep Picking   **Genre:** Metal

Music Description: In this example, pull-offs have been added to the sweep-picking exercise found in Week 43. As in that exercise, diatonic seventh chords in the key of A major descend strings 4–6 while simultaneously climbing the neck.

Tip: While performing the pull-offs, simultaneously jump your pick over string 4, moving it into place to perform the upward sweep of strings 5 and 6.

0:39

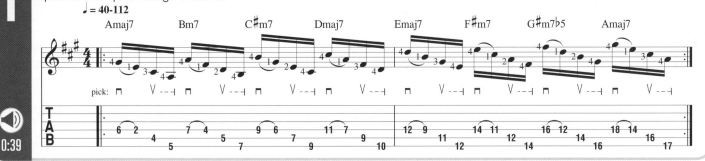

SAT

Exercise: #314   **Rhythm Tracks:** 9–16   **Technique:** Legato   **Genre:** Metal

Music Description: In this legato workout, the A harmonic minor scale (A–B–C–D–E–F–G#) descends all six strings via a sixteenth-note rhythm, pull-offs, and ascending and descending slides.

Tip: Although the slurs alternate between three- and five-note groupings, remember to count them as straight sixteenth notes. Notice that each pair of slurs fits within an eight-note, two beat span.

0:50

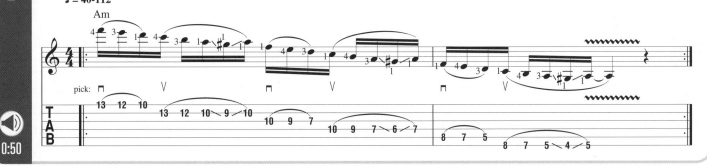

Exercise: #315   **Rhythm Tracks:** 1–8   **Technique:** Rhythm   **Genre:** Rock

Music Description: Hints of Jimi Hendrix can be heard in this chord-melody style rhythm, which, with the exception of the E major chord, utilizes sixth-string-rooted barre chords to outline the E–C#m7–B–A progression.

Tip: When voicing the B and A chords in measures 3 and 4, respectively, keep your index, middle, and ring fingers in place at all times, using only your pinky finger to play the chordal embellishments.

1:00

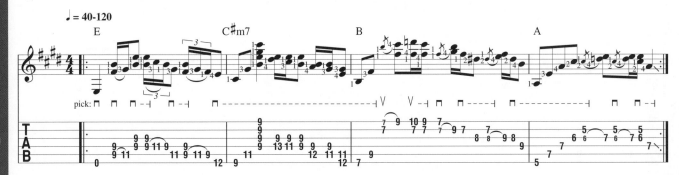

95

WEEK 46

EXERCISE TRACK 46

MON

Exercise: #316 **Rhythm Tracks:** 9–16 **Technique:** Alternate Picking **Genre:** Metal
Music Description: Like last Monday's exercise (#309), this figure is a straightforward sequence of the A harmonic minor scale, only this time the pattern descends.
Tip: To avoid confusion, focus intently on counting the rhythm rather than the scale's pattern and/or sound.

0:00

TUE

Exercise: #317 **Rhythm Tracks:** 25–32 **Technique:** String Skipping **Genre:** Jazz
Music Description: Like Exercise 310 from last Tuesday, this, too, is a snaky phrase that's played over a Gmaj7 chord. Here, strings 3, 4, and 5 are skipped during the line's descent.
Tip: For jazz authenticity, slide into the first note of the phrase.

0:11

WED

Exercise: #318 **Rhythm Tracks:** 33–40 **Technique:** String Bending **Genre:** Country
Music Description: A whole-step behind-the-nut bend and pre-bend, performed on strings 3 and 4, respectively, are combined with fretted notes to outline an A7 chord.
Tip: To execute the behind-the-nut bends, push down on the string (towards the headstock) with considerable pressure, using more than one finger, if necessary. If you can't coax a whole-step pre-bend from behind the nut, perform it as a fretted pre-bend at the fifth fret of string 5.

0:20

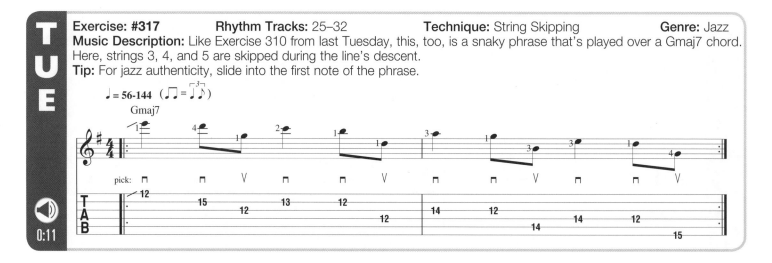

THU

Exercise: #319 **Rhythm Tracks:** 1–8 **Technique:** Arpeggios **Genre:** Rock
Music Description: This figure is the minor-arpeggio version of Exercise 305's sweep-picked barre chord.
Tip: Like last Thursday's exercise (#312), "roll" your ring (bar) finger to fret the notes on strings 4 and 3.

0:28

FRI

Exercise: #320 **Rhythm Tracks:** 9–16 **Technique:** Sweep Picking **Genre:** Metal
Music Description: A culmination of the sweep-picking exercises from the previous six weeks, this figure combines the familiar diatonic seventh-chord arpeggios (key of A) with down-sweeps, pull-offs, and sextuplet rhythms.
Tip: To help with the G#m7b5 chord's wide, five-fret stretch, leave your index finger off string 4 until the very moment your about to strike it. Your index finger should begin to approach the string while you're playing the note on string 5.

0:39

SAT

Exercise: #321 **Rhythm Tracks:** 9–16 **Technique:** Legato **Genre:** Metal
Music Description: Like last week's legato exercise (#314), the A harmonic minor scale provides the notes for this example, which combines ascending and descending slides and hammer-ons to climb all six strings. The festivities come to a climax with a seventeenth-fret finger tap of the root note, A.
Tip: Use the same finger pattern for each string pair (6–5, 4–3, and 2–1) and, to cap the phrase, articulate the tapped note with either the index finger or middle finger of your pick hand.

0:50

SUN

Exercise: #322 **Rhythm Tracks:** 25–32 **Technique:** Rhythm **Genre:** Jazz
Music Description: This jazz chord-melody exercise utilizes four-note adjacent-string chords to play a simple melody on string 1. Meanwhile, the Dm7–G7–Cmaj7 progression is reinforced by virtue of the various minor-, major-, and dominant-seventh chord inversions used in their respective measures.
Tip: To get the melody notes on string 1 to stand out among the other notes in the chord, use hybrid picking (a combination of your pick and fingers) and pluck the top string with slightly more force than the others.

1:00

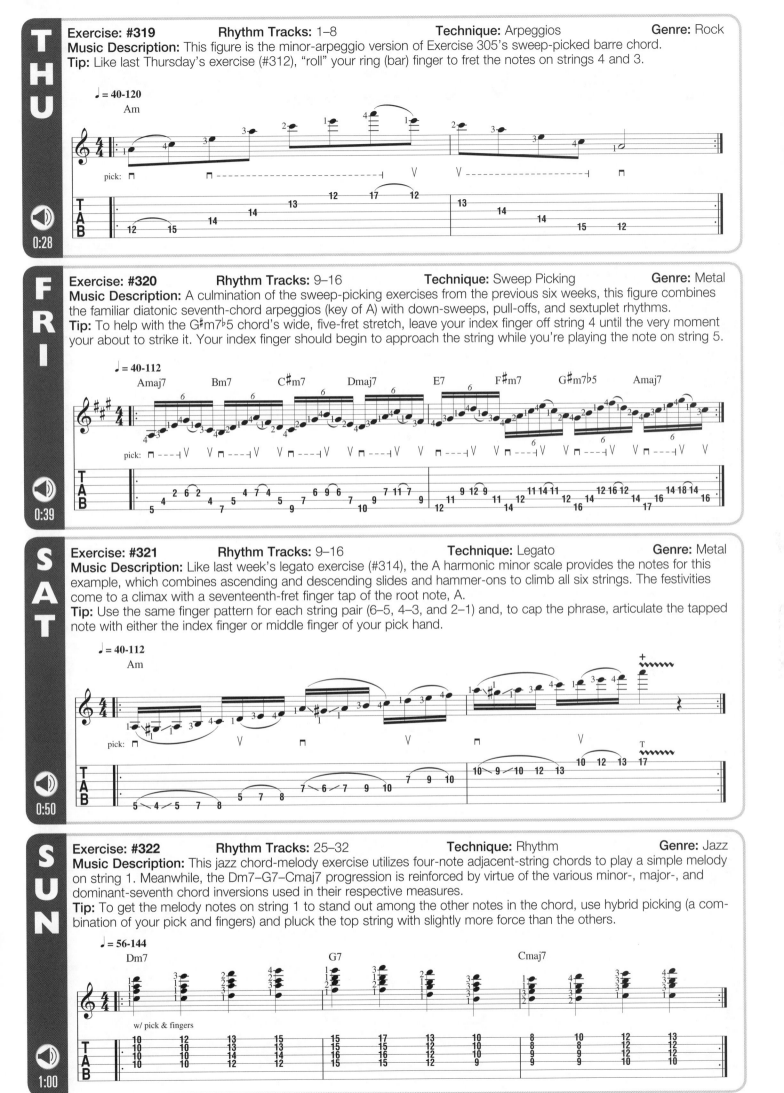

97

EXERCISE TRACK 47

MON

Exercise: #323 **Rhythm Tracks:** 9–16 **Technique:** Alternate Picking **Genre:** Metal
Music Description: This exercise combines the A harmonic minor scale with string skipping to produce a challenging alternate-picking sequence.
Tip: To facilitate the string skips, divide the sequence into six-note groupings (two strings, one skip), practicing each group multiple times before playing the exercise wholly.

0:00

TUE

Exercise: #324 **Rhythm Tracks:** 25–32 **Technique:** String Skipping **Genre:** Jazz
Music Description: This string-skipping lick, played over a V–ii progression (common in jazz) in C minor, weaves its way up an altered G scale in measure 1 before smoothly resolving to the root, C, in measure 2.
Tip: The notes in measure 2 are taken from the root-position C minor pentatonic scale and can be played exclusively with your fret-hand's index and ring fingers.

0:11

WED

Exercise: #325 **Rhythm Tracks:** 33–40 **Technique:** String Bending **Genre:** Country
Music Description: D7 and A7 chords are outlined with a combination of fretted notes and behind-the-nut whole-step bends and pre-bends.
Tip: Before commencing the phrase, place your pinky on the first fret of string 2 so that it's in place for the behind-the-nut bend in measure 1.

0:22

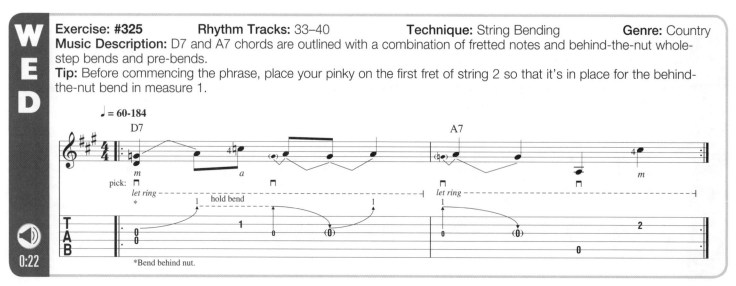

THU

Exercise: #326   **Rhythm Tracks:** 1–8   **Technique:** Arpeggios   **Genre:** Rock

Music Description: In this wild arpeggio workout, familiar A major barre-chord shapes are connected by a third chord voicing, resulting in an ascending/descending sweep-picking frenzy that climbs the neck.

Tip: To pull off this lick cleanly, closely follow the picking directions that are indicated between the notation and tab staves.

0:30

FRI

Exercise: #327   **Rhythm Tracks:** 9–16   **Technique:** Sweep Picking   **Genre:** Metal

Music Description: This sweep-picking exercise features multiple inversions of an E major triad (E–G♯–B–E, G♯–B–E–G♯, B–E–G♯–B, etc.) played in and around ninth position, in ascending and descending order.

Tip: Learn each inversion (four-note grouping) individually, and then string them together to form the entire phrase.

0:40

SAT

Exercise: #328   **Rhythm Tracks:** 9–16   **Technique:** Legato   **Genre:** Metal

Music Description: This legato line borrows elements from Exercises 314 and 321, such as the A harmonic minor scale, but adds an exciting twist: an ascending and descending slide of the tapping finger on string 1.

Tip: When you pull off from string 1 with your tapping finger, after you've performed the slides, don't just lift the finger off the fretboard; instead, bend it slightly sharp (towards the ceiling or floor) while simultaneously releasing pressure on the string. This will maintain a consistent attack volume for all nine notes of the slur.

0:52

SUN

Exercise: #329   **Rhythm Tracks:** 25–32   **Technique:** Rhythm   **Genre:** Jazz

Music Description: In this rhythm workout, the jazz chord melody from last Sunday (#322) is transferred from strings 1–4 to strings 2–5, shifting the notes down one octave and necessitating new chord voicings.

Tip: Once you're comfortable playing this figure as written, turn it into an eighth-note example by restating the melody notes (string 2) after each chord. This will prep you for what's to come next Sunday (#336).

1:03

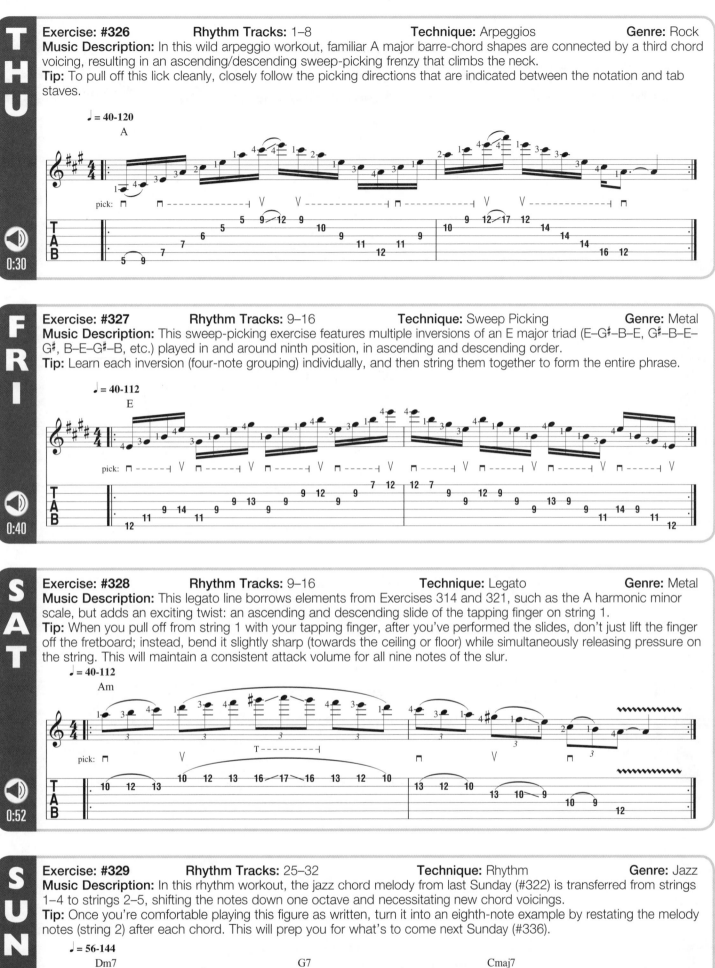

EXERCISE TRACK 48

MON

Exercise: #330   **Rhythm Tracks:** 9–16   **Technique:** Alternate Picking   **Genre:** Metal
Music Description: This exercise continues the concepts that were introduced last Monday (#323), only this time in descending fashion.
Tip: The notes played after the string skips are one octave lower than the notes preceding the skips; therefore, let the sound of the notes help guide your fret hand.

0:00

TUE

Exercise: #331   **Rhythm Tracks:** 9–16   **Technique:** String Skipping   **Genre:** Metal
Music Description: The G diminished scale supplies the notes for this string-skipping finger-stretcher in twelfth position.
Tip: The same fingering is used on both strings (first and third) in this exercise, so spend extra time getting the pattern under your fingers before attacking the entire phrase.

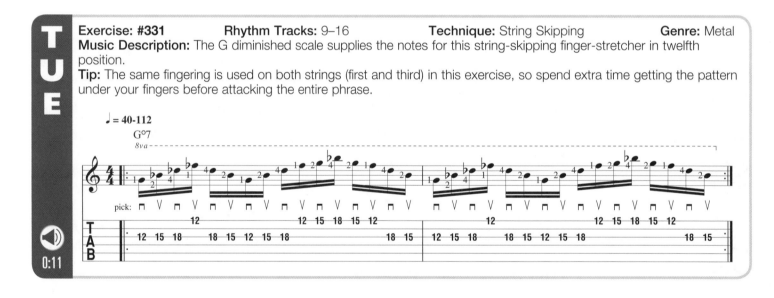

0:11

WED

Exercise: #332   **Rhythm Tracks:** 33–40   **Technique:** String Bending   **Genre:** Country
Music Description: An oblique pre-bend on strings 1 and 2, a double-stop (i.e., double-string) pre-bend with multiple intervals (half and whole steps) on strings 2 and 3, and a double-stop pre-bend with unison intervals on strings 3 and 4 are highlights of this A dominant-seventh lick.
Tip: After the first-measure oblique bend, the rest of the phrase fits nicely in fifth position.

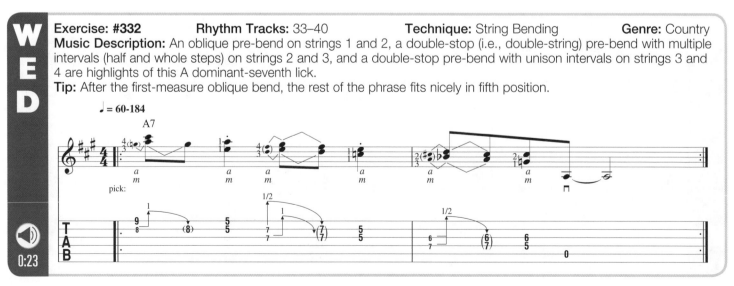

0:23

THU 0:31

Exercise: #333   **Rhythm Tracks:** 1–8   **Technique:** Arpeggios   **Genre:** Rock

Music Description: This example is the minor version of the arpeggio exercise from last week (#326). The chord's 3rd degree, C♯, has been lowered a half step, or one fret, to C natural.

Tip: Keep a close eye on your pinky as your fret hand slides up string 1, using it as a guide to find the stops at frets 12 and 17.

FRI 0:42

Exercise: #334   **Rhythm Tracks:** 25–32   **Technique:** Sweep Picking   **Genre:** Jazz

Music Description: This jagged jazz line features the G altered scale played over (what else?) an altered G chord (e.g., G7♯5, G7♭5), with eighth-note triplets supplying the rhythm for each sweep.

Tip: In measure 1, use a middle-finger bar on the fourth-fret notes on beat 2 and, on beat 4, an index-finger bar for those same notes.

SAT 0:52

Exercise: #335   **Rhythm Tracks:** 9–16   **Technique:** Legato   **Genre:** Metal

Music Description: This figure expands on the ideas introduced in Exercises 314, 321, and 328. Specifically, the A harmonic minor scale is combined with hammer-ons, pull-offs, and ascending/descending tapping-finger slides to form a slippery lower-string legato line.

Tip: Position your pick hand close to the eleventh position so that it doesn't necessitate a large jump to execute the taps and slides. It's perfectly acceptable to pick the strings over the neck area, rather than over the pickups.

SUN 1:04

Exercise: #336   **Rhythm Tracks:** 25–32   **Technique:** Rhythm   **Genre:** Jazz

Music Description: The Dm7–G7–Cmaj7 progression from Exercises 322 and 329 has been retained for this jazz rhythm workout; however, the melody is more sophisticated in this example, and the rhythm has been cranked up a notch, from quarter notes to eighth notes.

Tip: The proper pick-hand technique to use in this figure is to alternate between "pulling" the chords with a combination of your pick and fingers and using an upstroke with your ring or pinky finger for the additional melody notes on the "and" of each beat.

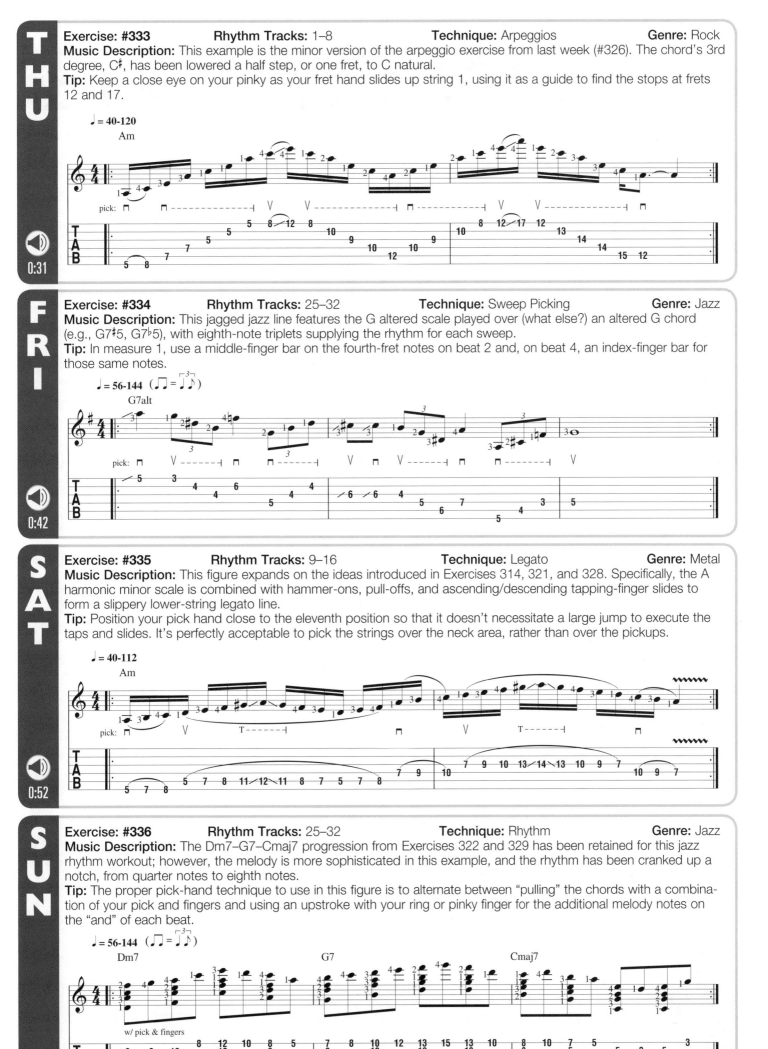

MON

Exercise: #337   **Rhythm Tracks:** 25–32   **Technique:** Alternate Picking   **Genre:** Jazz

Music Description: Another challenging alternate-picking workout, this bebop line features a chord sequence made famous by saxophonist John Coltrane, navigated with four-note minor, major, and dominant seventh arpeggios.

Tip: Because this is a jazz line, the eighth notes should be swung. (In each two-note pair, the first note should be played slightly longer than the second.)

0:00

TUE

Exercise: #338   **Rhythm Tracks:** 9–16   **Technique:** String Skipping   **Genre:** Metal

Music Description: Based entirely in the E natural minor scale, this string-skipping exercise revolves around a six-note sequence primarily on the third string, with notes introduced intermittently on the first string.

Tip: Bar strings 1–3 with your pinky to access the high E note (first string, fret 12) on beat 2 of the second measure.

0:13

WED

Exercise: #339   **Rhythm Tracks:** 33–40   **Technique:** String Bending   **Genre:** Country

Music Description: A7, G7, and D7 chords are outlined with a phrase that features whole-step bends and pre-bends on string 3. The line is initially played in twelfth position, and then restated in tenth and fifth positions.

Tip: While you're playing the first note of each measure, pre-bend the second note of the measure, preparing it for performance.

0:24

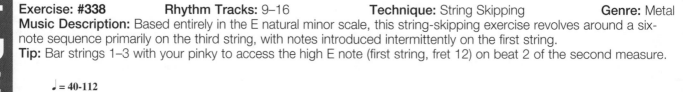

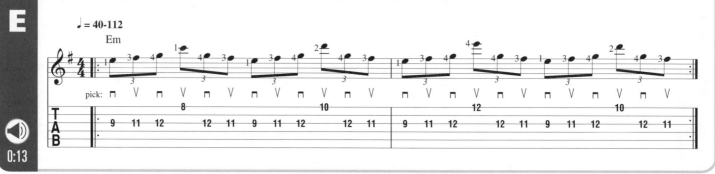

THU

0:35

Exercise: #340   **Rhythm Tracks:** 1–8   **Technique:** Arpeggios   **Genre:** Rock

Music Description: Am, C, G, and Em arpeggios move about the neck in an ascending/descending pattern via familiar sixth-string-rooted major and minor barre-chord shapes.

Tip: Sweep picking reigns supreme in this arpeggio exercise. For best results, follow the picking directions notated between staves.

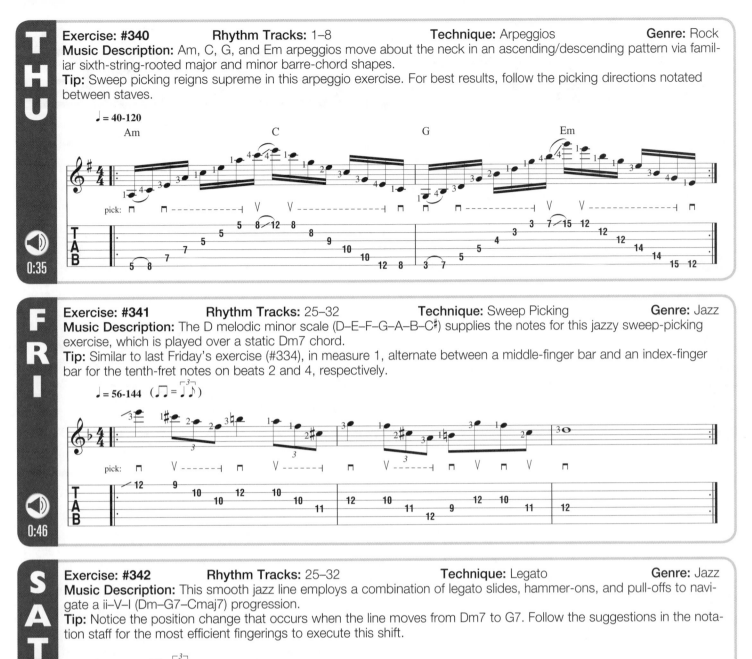

FRI

0:46

Exercise: #341   **Rhythm Tracks:** 25–32   **Technique:** Sweep Picking   **Genre:** Jazz

Music Description: The D melodic minor scale (D–E–F–G–A–B–C♯) supplies the notes for this jazzy sweep-picking exercise, which is played over a static Dm7 chord.

Tip: Similar to last Friday's exercise (#334), in measure 1, alternate between a middle-finger bar and an index-finger bar for the tenth-fret notes on beats 2 and 4, respectively.

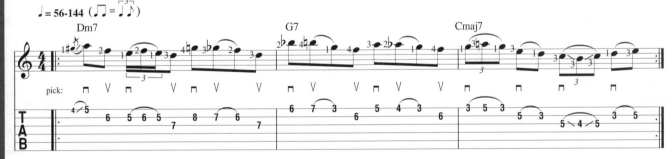

SAT

0:56

Exercise: #342   **Rhythm Tracks:** 25–32   **Technique:** Legato   **Genre:** Jazz

Music Description: This smooth jazz line employs a combination of legato slides, hammer-ons, and pull-offs to navigate a ii–V–I (Dm–G7–Cmaj7) progression.

Tip: Notice the position change that occurs when the line moves from Dm7 to G7. Follow the suggestions in the notation staff for the most efficient fingerings to execute this shift.

SUN

1:08

Exercise: #343   **Rhythm Tracks:** 25–32   **Technique:** Rhythm   **Genre:** Jazz

Music Description: A steady quarter-note walking bass line, interspersed with minor-, major-, and dominant-seventh chord inversions, navigates a Gm7–C7–Fmaj7 progression.

Tip: Use hybrid picking throughout this figure, plucking the bass notes with a downstroke of your pick and "pulling" the chords with a combination of your pick and middle, ring, and pinky fingers.

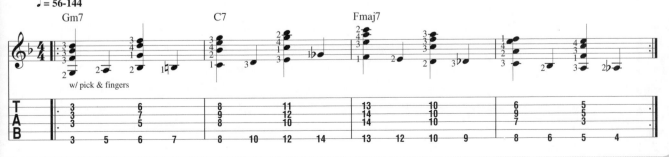

WEEK 50

EXERCISE TRACK 50

MON

Exercise: #344   **Rhythm Tracks:** 25–32   **Technique:** Alternate Picking   **Genre:** Jazz

Music Description: This line features the same Dm7–E♭7–A♭maj7–B7–Emaj7–G7–Cmaj7 progression as last Monday (#337); however, the sequence of ascending and descending arpeggios is reversed.

Tip: Swing the eighth notes and, for greatest efficiency, follow the fingering suggestions in the notation staff for greatest efficiency.

0:00

TUE

Exercise: #345   **Rhythm Tracks:** 9–16   **Technique:** String Skipping   **Genre:** Metal

Music Description: Rooted in the C major scale and arranged in a three-notes-per-string pattern, this shred line offers both two-string (ascending) and one-string (descending) skips.

Tip: Notice that strings 5–6 share the same finger pattern, as do strings 3–4 and strings 1–2.

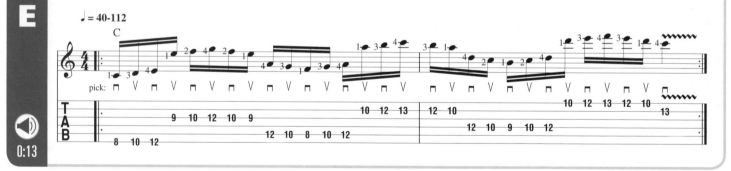

0:13

WED

Exercise: #346   **Rhythm Tracks:** 33–40   **Technique:** String Bending   **Genre:** Country

Music Description: Triads from the D7 family of chords are arranged in descending fashion along strings 1–3 and voiced with various whole- and half-step bends.

Tip: There are multiple ways to finger this phrase; however, use the fingerings indicated below the tab staff as guidelines.

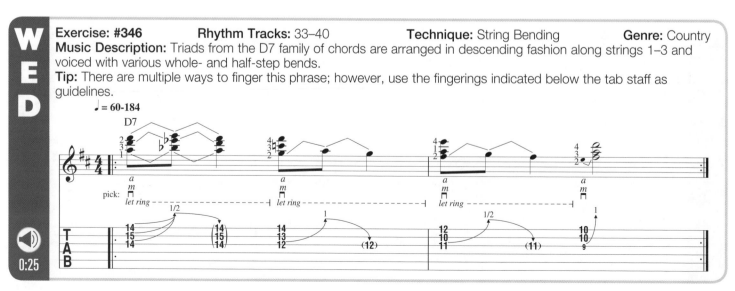

0:25

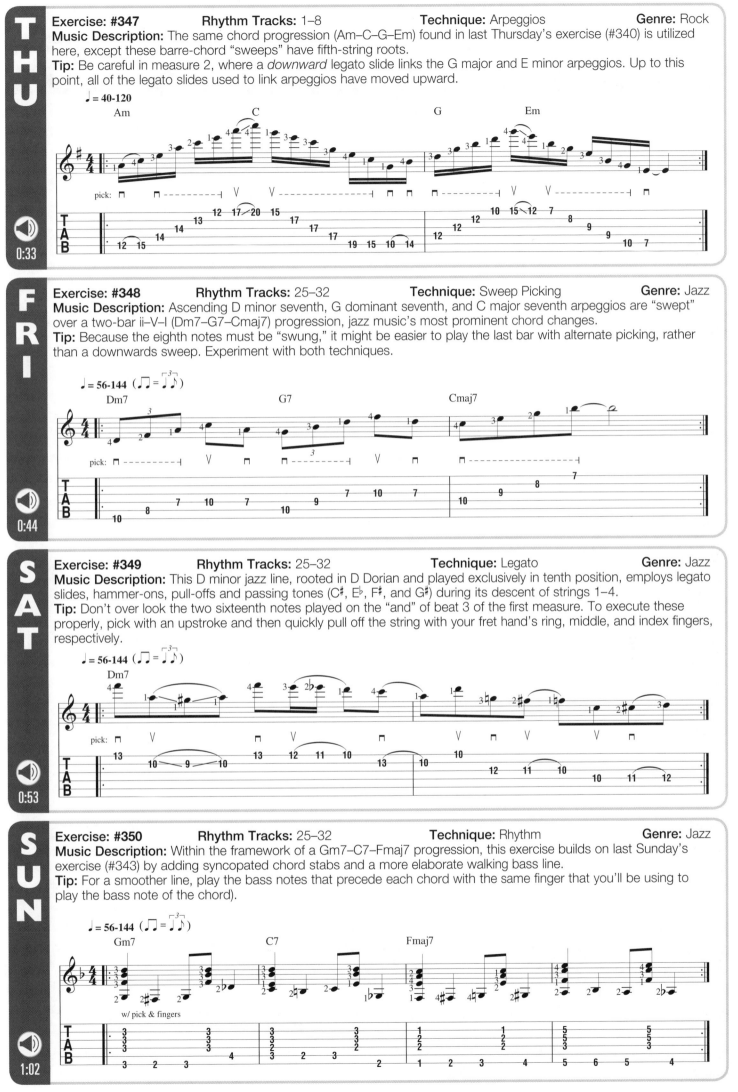

THU

0:33

Exercise: #347   **Rhythm Tracks:** 1–8   **Technique:** Arpeggios   **Genre:** Rock

Music Description: The same chord progression (Am–C–G–Em) found in last Thursday's exercise (#340) is utilized here, except these barre-chord "sweeps" have fifth-string roots.

Tip: Be careful in measure 2, where a *downward* legato slide links the G major and E minor arpeggios. Up to this point, all of the legato slides used to link arpeggios have moved upward.

FRI

0:44

Exercise: #348   **Rhythm Tracks:** 25–32   **Technique:** Sweep Picking   **Genre:** Jazz

Music Description: Ascending D minor seventh, G dominant seventh, and C major seventh arpeggios are "swept" over a two-bar ii–V–I (Dm7–G7–Cmaj7) progression, jazz music's most prominent chord changes.

Tip: Because the eighth notes must be "swung," it might be easier to play the last bar with alternate picking, rather than a downwards sweep. Experiment with both techniques.

SAT

0:53

Exercise: #349   **Rhythm Tracks:** 25–32   **Technique:** Legato   **Genre:** Jazz

Music Description: This D minor jazz line, rooted in D Dorian and played exclusively in tenth position, employs legato slides, hammer-ons, pull-offs and passing tones (C♯, E♭, F♯, and G♯) during its descent of strings 1–4.

Tip: Don't over look the two sixteenth notes played on the "and" of beat 3 of the first measure. To execute these properly, pick with an upstroke and then quickly pull off the string with your fret hand's ring, middle, and index fingers, respectively.

SUN

1:02

Exercise: #350   **Rhythm Tracks:** 25–32   **Technique:** Rhythm   **Genre:** Jazz

Music Description: Within the framework of a Gm7–C7–Fmaj7 progression, this exercise builds on last Sunday's exercise (#343) by adding syncopated chord stabs and a more elaborate walking bass line.

Tip: For a smoother line, play the bass notes that precede each chord with the same finger that you'll be using to play the bass note of the chord).

GUITAR

AEROBICS

WEEK 51

EXERCISE TRACK 51

MON

Exercise: #351   **Rhythm Tracks:** 25–32   **Technique:** Alternate Picking   **Genre:** Jazz

Music Description: This three-bar ii–V–i progression is in the key of G minor and features an uninterrupted stream of eighth notes—a great alternate-picking exercise—that outline the chord changes.

Tip: Once you're comfortable starting the exercise with a downstroke, using alternate-picking throughout, reverse the pattern and begin the line with an upstroke.

0:00

TUE

Exercise: #352   **Rhythm Tracks:** 9–16   **Technique:** String Skipping   **Genre:** Metal

Music Description: This figure is the descending version of last week's string-skipping exercise (#345).

Tip: The three-notes-per-string sequence of the line works against the four-note groupings of each beat, presenting a rhythmic challenge. So take extra reps at the slower tempos before cranking up the tempo!

0:11

WED

Exercise: #353   **Rhythm Tracks:** 33–40   **Technique:** String Bending   **Genre:** Country

Music Description: This arpeggiated figure, which works great as a tag at the end of a tune, features whole-step bends and releases on string 3 of each chord.

Tip: For the first three chords (A/E, B9/E, and Bm9/E), your index and pinky fingers should remain fixed on strings 3 and 4, respectively, while your ring and middle fingers fret the descending notes on string 5.

0:22

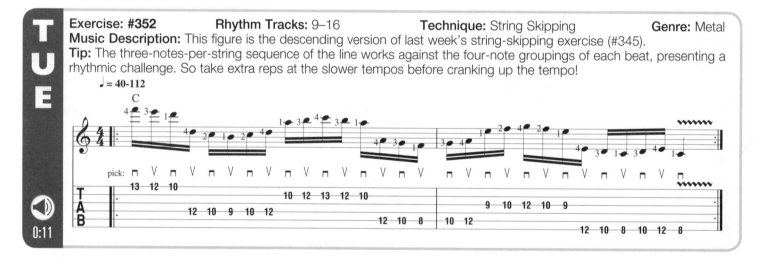

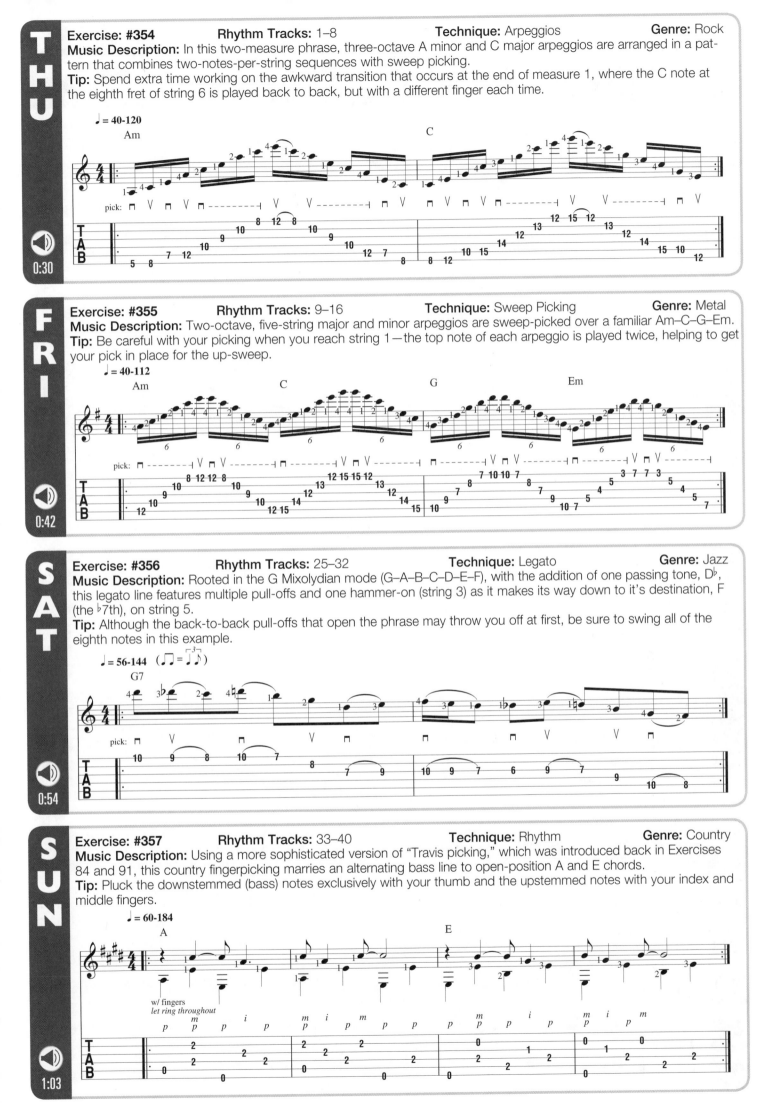

THU

Exercise: #354 **Rhythm Tracks:** 1–8 **Technique:** Arpeggios **Genre:** Rock

Music Description: In this two-measure phrase, three-octave A minor and C major arpeggios are arranged in a pattern that combines two-notes-per-string sequences with sweep picking.

Tip: Spend extra time working on the awkward transition that occurs at the end of measure 1, where the C note at the eighth fret of string 6 is played back to back, but with a different finger each time.

0:30

FRI

Exercise: #355 **Rhythm Tracks:** 9–16 **Technique:** Sweep Picking **Genre:** Metal

Music Description: Two-octave, five-string major and minor arpeggios are sweep-picked over a familiar Am–C–G–Em.

Tip: Be careful with your picking when you reach string 1—the top note of each arpeggio is played twice, helping to get your pick in place for the up-sweep.

0:42

SAT

Exercise: #356 **Rhythm Tracks:** 25–32 **Technique:** Legato **Genre:** Jazz

Music Description: Rooted in the G Mixolydian mode (G–A–B–C–D–E–F), with the addition of one passing tone, D♭, this legato line features multiple pull-offs and one hammer-on (string 3) as it makes its way down to it's destination, F (the ♭7th), on string 5.

Tip: Although the back-to-back pull-offs that open the phrase may throw you off at first, be sure to swing all of the eighth notes in this example.

0:54

SUN

Exercise: #357 **Rhythm Tracks:** 33–40 **Technique:** Rhythm **Genre:** Country

Music Description: Using a more sophisticated version of "Travis picking," which was introduced back in Exercises 84 and 91, this country fingerpicking marries an alternating bass line to open-position A and E chords.

Tip: Pluck the downstemmed (bass) notes exclusively with your thumb and the upstemmed notes with your index and middle fingers.

1:03

EXERCISE TRACK 52

MON

Exercise: #358 **Rhythm Tracks:** 25–32 **Technique:** Alternate Picking **Genre:** Jazz

Music Description: Similar to a blues turnaround (last two bars of a 12-bar blues), this Imaj7–VI7–iim7–V7 jazz turn-around incorporates both scalar lines and arpeggios to navigate the progression, making for a great alternate-picking exercise.

Tip: This entire phrase is played in fifth position. For best results, follow the suggested fingerings that are located in the notation staff.

♩ = 56-144

0:00

TUE

Exercise: #359 **Rhythm Tracks:** 9–16 **Technique:** String Skipping **Genre:** Metal

Music Description: To cap this book's string-skipping exercises, here's a jaw-dropping—and nearly impossible—sequence of E minor arpeggios played on strings 1, 4, and 6. For proof that this lick can be performed—and at blazing speed, no less—check out Paul Gilbert's *Intense Rock* video.

Tip: Practice this exercise *slowly*!

♩ = 40-112

0:11

WED

Exercise: #360 **Rhythm Tracks:** 33–40 **Technique:** String Bending **Genre:** Country

Music Description: This country chord melody is played on strings 3–5 exclusively and features a handful of whole-step bends.

Tip: Assign your pick, middle finger, and ringer finger to strings 5, 4, and 3, respectively. Use this combination to pick the entire phrase.

♩ = 60-184

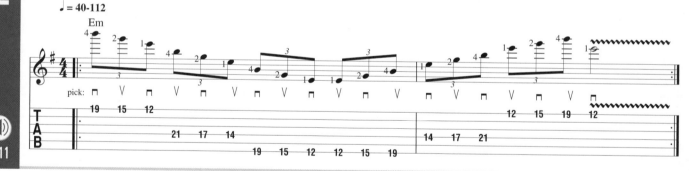

0:22

THU

Exercise: #361 **Rhythm Tracks:** 1–8 **Technique:** Arpeggios **Genre:** Rock

Music Description: The two-notes-per-string/sweep-picking pattern from last Thursday (#354) is retained here for the G major arpeggio. The E minor arpeggio, however, starts on the chord's 5th degree, B, and utilizes a one-note/two-notes pattern for each string pair (6–5, 4–3, and 2–1).

Tip: For the E minor arpeggio, a single three-note finger pattern can be used for all three string pairs. This pattern will tempt you to play triplets, but sixteenth notes should be maintained throughout the phrase.

0:33

FRI

Exercise: #362 **Rhythm Tracks:** 9–16 **Technique:** Sweep Picking **Genre:** Metal

Music Description: The Am–C–G–Em progression from last Friday's sweep-picking exercise (#355) are back; this time, however, the arpeggios alternate between down- and up-sweeps on each chord change.

Tip: Shifting down the neck to perform an upward sweep (measure 2) is considerably more difficult than moving up the neck (measure 1), so spend extra time working on the transition from the G arpeggio to the Em arpeggio.

0:44

SAT

Exercise: #363 **Rhythm Tracks:** 25–32 **Technique:** Legato **Genre:** Jazz

Music Description: A three-note motif, restated twice, supplies the melodic fabric for this C major legato line that features pull-offs on strings 1 and 2, a hammer-on on string 3, and a slide that resolves to the root, C, on string 4.

Tip: This figure is pinky free! The entire phrase can be played exclusively with your fret hand's index, middle and ring fingers. Follow the fingerings in the notation staff for best results.

0:55

SUN

Exercise: #364 **Rhythm Tracks:** 33–40 **Technique:** Rhythm **Genre:** Country

Music Description: Famed guitar picker Chet Atkins made this type of "Travis picking" figure a staple of country music. Here, a fifth-string-rooted D major barre chord and a sixth-string-rooted A major barre chord provide the notes for the fingerpicking festivities.

Tip: For the A major chord, keep your index, middle, and ring fingers planted on the fretboard at all times, using your pinky to play the descending melody on string 2.

1:04

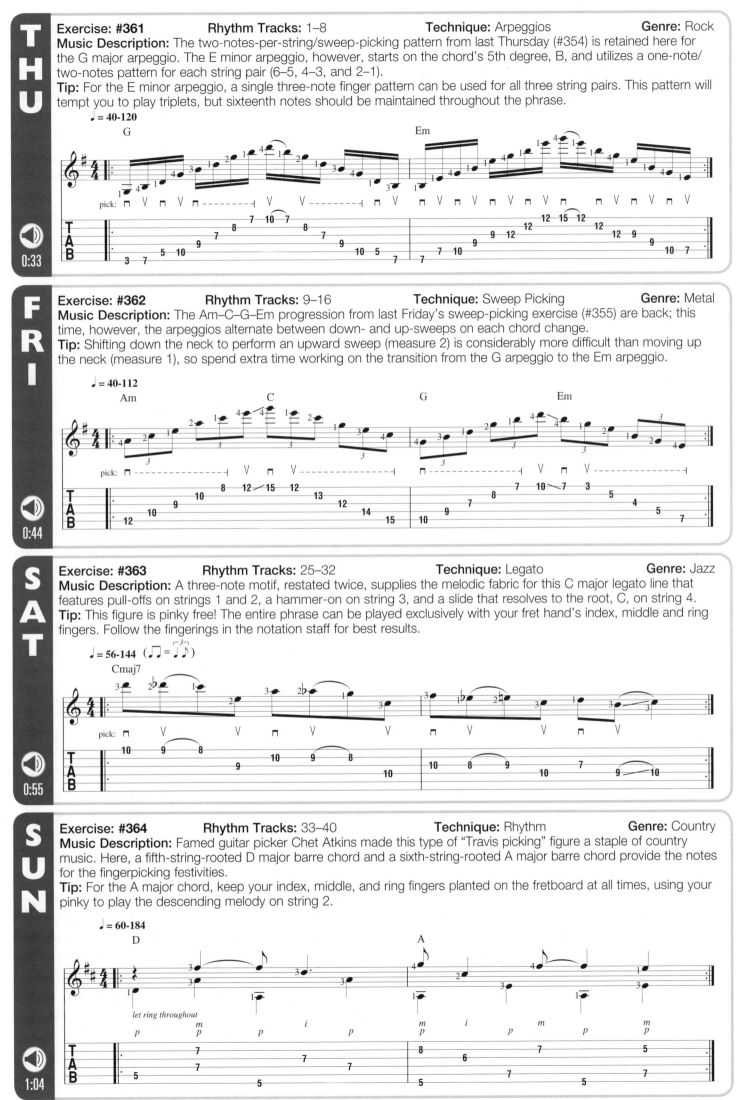

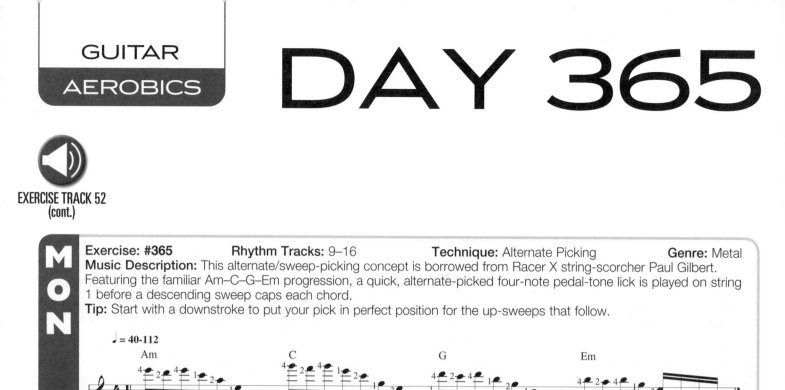

ACKNOWLEDGMENTS

This book is dedicated to my sister, Tonia, for tolerating the racket that emanated from my bedroom during my developmental stages as a guitarist; to my parents, Don and Sonja Nelson, for their unconditional love and support while I pursued a career in the uncertain music industry; and especially to my wife, Amy, who offered constant encouragement throughout this project, and my twin daughters, Sophie and Claire, who were born during the writing of *Guitar Aerobics*.

I'd also like to thank all of the musicians, past and present, who have inspired and influenced me throughout the years.

ABOUT THE AUTHOR

Troy Nelson is a 20-year veteran of the six-string. First picking up the instrument during the heyday of "hair metal," some of his first guitar heroes included George Lynch, Paul Gilbert, and Nuno Bettencourt. After high school, he studied jazz guitar for two years at Milwaukee Area Technical College, where his musical influences expanded to include Charlie Parker, John Coltrane, and Wes Montgomery, among others. In 1994, he began his relationship with Hal Leonard, for whom he has edited, proofread, and transcribed numerous guitar publications. One of those projects included *Guitar One*, a magazine the company launched in 1995. While at the magazine, Nelson held the titles of Music Editor, Senior Editor, and Editor-in-Chief. After a decade at the magazine, he resigned from *Guitar One* to pursue his other love, football. He spent the 2005 NFL season with the New York Jets, during which time he wrote all of the team's gameday stories, as well as numerous player features, fantasy football previews, and NFL Draft scouting reports. Later that year, however, Hal Leonard launched *Guitar Edge* magazine and lured Nelson back to the music biz as its Senior Editor, a title he holds today. Nelson currently resides in Athens, Georgia, with his wife, Amy, and twin daughters, Sophie and Claire. When he's not busy playing guitar or changing diapers, he attends classes at the University of Georgia, home of the Bulldogs!

GUITAR NOTATION LEGEND

Guitar music can be notated three different ways: on a *musical staff*, in *tablature*, and in *rhythm slashes*.

RHYTHM SLASHES are written above the staff. Strum chords in the rhythm indicated. Use the chord diagrams found at the top of the first page of the transcription for the appropriate chord voicings. Round noteheads indicate single notes.

THE MUSICAL STAFF shows pitches and rhythms and is divided by bar lines into measures. Pitches are named after the first seven letters of the alphabet.

TABLATURE graphically represents the guitar fingerboard. Each horizontal line represents a string, and each number represents a fret.

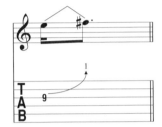

4th string, 2nd fret | 1st & 2nd strings open, played together | open D chord

DEFINITIONS FOR SPECIAL GUITAR NOTATION

HALF-STEP BEND: Strike the note and bend up 1/2 step.

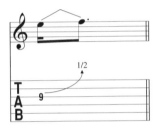

WHOLE-STEP BEND: Strike the note and bend up one step.

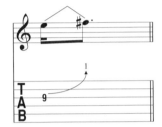

GRACE NOTE BEND: Strike the note and immediately bend up as indicated.

SLIGHT (MICROTONE) BEND: Strike the note and bend up 1/4 step.

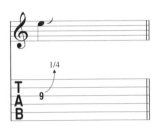

BEND AND RELEASE: Strike the note and bend up as indicated, then release back to the original note. Only the first note is struck.

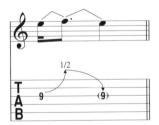

PRE-BEND: Bend the note as indicated, then strike it.

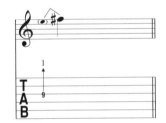

PRE-BEND AND RELEASE: Bend the note as indicated. Strike it and release the bend back to the original note.

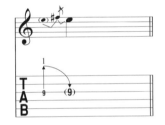

UNISON BEND: Strike the two notes simultaneously and bend the lower note up to the pitch of the higher.

VIBRATO: The string is vibrated by rapidly bending and releasing the note with the fretting hand.

WIDE VIBRATO: The pitch is varied to a greater degree by vibrating with the fretting hand.

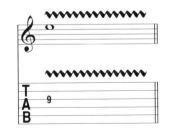

HAMMER-ON: Strike the first (lower) note with one finger, then sound the higher note (on the same string) with another finger by fretting it without picking.

PULL-OFF: Place both fingers on the notes to be sounded. Strike the first note and without picking, pull the finger off to sound the second (lower) note.

LEGATO SLIDE: Strike the first note and then slide the same fret-hand finger up or down to the second note. The second note is not struck.

SHIFT SLIDE: Same as legato slide, except the second note is struck.

TRILL: Very rapidly alternate between the notes indicated by continuously hammering on and pulling off.

TAPPING: Hammer ("tap") the fret indicated with the pick-hand index or middle finger and pull off to the note fretted by the fret hand.

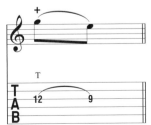

111

NATURAL HARMONIC: Strike the note while the fret-hand lightly touches the string directly over the fret indicated.

PINCH HARMONIC: The note is fretted normally and a harmonic is produced by adding the edge of the thumb or the tip of the index finger of the pick hand to the normal pick attack.

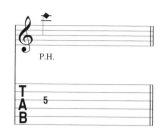

HARP HARMONIC: The note is fretted normally and a harmonic is produced by gently resting the pick hand's index finger directly above the indicated fret (in parentheses) while the pick hand's thumb or pick assists by plucking the appropriate string.

PICK SCRAPE: The edge of the pick is rubbed down (or up) the string, producing a scratchy sound.

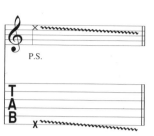

MUFFLED STRINGS: A percussive sound is produced by laying the fret hand across the string(s) without depressing, and striking them with the pick hand.

PALM MUTING: The note is partially muted by the pick hand lightly touching the string(s) just before the bridge.

RAKE: Drag the pick across the strings indicated with a single motion.

TREMOLO PICKING: The note is picked as rapidly and continuously as possible.

ARPEGGIATE: Play the notes of the chord indicated by quickly rolling them from bottom to top.

VIBRATO BAR DIVE AND RETURN: The pitch of the note or chord is dropped a specified number of steps (in rhythm), then returned to the original pitch.

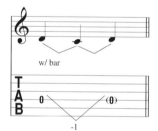

VIBRATO BAR SCOOP: Depress the bar just before striking the note, then quickly release the bar.

VIBRATO BAR DIP: Strike the note and then immediately drop a specified number of steps, then release back to the original pitch.

ADDITIONAL MUSICAL DEFINITIONS

>	(accent)	• Accentuate note (play it louder).
^	(accent)	• Accentuate note with great intensity.
.	(staccato)	• Play the note short.
⊓		• Downstroke
V		• Upstroke
D.S. al Coda		• Go back to the sign (%), then play until the measure marked "*To Coda*," then skip to the section labelled "**Coda**."
D.C. al Fine		• Go back to the beginning of the song and play until the measure marked "*Fine*" (end).

Rhy. Fig.	• Label used to recall a recurring accompaniment pattern (usually chordal).
Riff	• Label used to recall composed, melodic lines (usually single notes) which recur.
Fill	• Label used to identify a brief melodic figure which is to be inserted into the arrangement.
Rhy. Fill	• A chordal version of a Fill.
tacet	• Instrument is silent (drops out).
	• Repeat measures between signs.
	• When a repeated section has different endings, play the first ending only the first time and the second ending only the second time.

NOTE: Tablature numbers in parentheses mean:
1. The note is being sustained over a system (note in standard notation is tied), or
2. The note is sustained, but a new articulation (such as a hammer-on, pull-off, slide or vibrato) begins, or
3. The note is a barely audible "ghost" note (note in standard notation is also in parentheses).